POLICY STUDIES IN EMPLOYMENT AND WELFARE NUMBER 6

General Editors: Sar A. Levitan and Garth L. Mangum

The Conscience
of the Corporations:
Business and Urban
Affairs, 1967-1970

Jules Cohn

The Johns Hopkins Press, Baltimore and London

The Johns Hopkins Press, Baltimore, Maryland 21218
The Johns Hopkins Press Ltd., London

Library of Congress Catalog Card Number 77-135533

ISBN (clothbound) 0-8018-1231-3
ISBN (paperbound) 0-8018-1230-5

Parts of this book appeared originally, in different form, in the *Harvard Business Review*, March-April 1970, *Urban Affairs Quarterly*, September 1970, and *Social Policy*, April-May 1970.

For Barbara Joy

"The battle with the slum began the day civilization recognized in it her enemy. It was a losing fight until conscience joined forces with fear and self-interest against it. When common sense and the golden rule obtain among men as a rule of practice, it will be over."

Jacob Riis, *A Ten Years' War* (1900)

Contents

Preface

This book provides a chronicle and analysis of big business's recent efforts to relieve urban problems. After the first wave of riots in the nation's cities in the summer of 1967, one major corporation after another announced that it would undertake urban affairs programs. An anxious, alarmed, and angry public was assured that businessmen would come to the aid of government and voluntary welfare agencies, and that industry's management know-how as well as some of its capital and technological resources would be mobilized in the battle to improve life in the cities. Jobs and training for the hard core of the poor would be provided, and other programs would be devised to meet the needs of minority group members, particularly blacks.

The ability and willingness of the private sector to carry out its pledges has been a subject of controversy ever since the first high-minded pronouncements were issued from executive suites. Though four years have passed since those pronouncements were made, the problems that they addressed are still with us. What have corporate urban affairs programs amounted to? What have been the effects in large companies of special programs for the disadvantaged? What has been learned about the ability of corporate leaders to comprehend and do something about society's problems?

Has the private sector shown that it can play a useful role in today's community welfare efforts? Can any lesson be drawn for makers of public policy, urban crisis-watchers, and businessmen about the positive potentialities as well as the hazards inherent in corporate urban affairs programs?

Answers to the above and related questions are offered in the chapters that follow. This book is divided into three parts: Chapters 1 through 6 report on my nationwide study of corporate programs, conducted in two phases, from June to November 1969, and April to July 1970. Two hundred and forty-seven companies were included in the study sample: commercial banks; life insurance, retailing, and transportation companies; utilities; and industrial companies (heavy manufacturing, light manufacturing, petroleum, aerospace, electronics, office equipment, and others), all of which appear on *Fortune's* lists of the largest American corporations. Top executives and their assistants in 186 of these companies were interviewed in person; information was obtained in correspondence and questionnaires from the remaining 61 companies. The study sought to obtain quantitative as well as qualitative findings about industry's efforts, and frank appraisal rather than mere rhetoric from respondents. Top managers were asked to comment on such topics as the types of effort underway; numbers of people hired trained, and promoted; the progress of programs; dollar costs; and prospects for the future. The most popular types of urban affairs programs were examined in detail. In addition, data were obtained about the organizational status of urban affairs activities and the men (or women) administering them.

Chapter 7 provides a case study of a subsidiary created by one large company to provide jobs and training for people heretofore considered unemployable. The case identifies some of the complex issues that develop when conscience-stricken businessmen decide to grapple with social problems. Facts and figures were obtained in a six-month study of the subsidiary, including a series of on-site visits and interviews. Students, or others who have had no first-hand experience with the urban affairs efforts of business, might find it useful to read the case study first, and then turn to the other chapters. For businessmen interested in meeting the challenges presented by programs for the disadvantaged, Part II concludes by suggesting some guidelines for effective action.

Chapter 8 offers conclusions based on the nationwide survey and the case study. It identifies and assesses the major issues that arise when executives respond to business problems, on the one hand, and to the call of the corporate conscience, on the other.

I am indebted to friends and colleagues for services that only friendly colleagues can render—criticism, suggestions, and encouragement. Roland Mann made helpful comments on an early draft of the manuscript. Maxine Nord assisted in the research design and the tabulation of data. To Aileen Kyte I owe special thanks and appreciation for saving me from a number of errors of fact and judgment. The opinions expressed in this book are my own, but I would like to acknowledge support and services provided by McKinsey and Company, Inc. I also thank Annabelle Devine and Joan Jacobs for meeting my production deadlines not only efficiently but cordially, and Barbara Miller for providing editorial services. Finally, I thank Sar A. Levitan for inviting me to contribute to this series.

The Conscience of the Corporations:
Business and Urban Affairs, 1967–1970

1

The Picture Today: An Overview

In the aftermath of riots in Watts, Detroit, and Newark, the conscience of the corporations sought expression through hundreds of urban affairs programs across the nation. After four years, it is clear that conscience alone will not be enough to sustain corporate efforts to relieve the problems of the cities. Many businessmen freely acknowledge dissatisfaction with their accomplishments thus far and say they ran into more setbacks and snags than they anticipated. Others announce that they have cut back their funding of programs and are having second thoughts about the nature of the role they should play in community service. Most of the board chairmen and company presidents interviewed seem chastened by their experiences as urban do-gooders, as though they had passed through some exotic rites of initiation and are now looking back, trying to understand what happened and why.

Declining profits caused by the economic recession of 1970–71 have imposed heavy constraints on all corporate activities and provide sound business reasons for calling a halt to any lavish demonstration of the corporate conscience, at least for the time being. With dollar costs to worry about, as well as organizational strains and stresses that flow from urban affairs activities, many companies are pausing before extending their commitments. There is more inclination to evaluate the past than to take on new challenges. And the waning of interest on the part of some companies is demonstrated daily by announcements of the termination of training programs for the disadvantaged and layoffs of unskilled workers.

Most businessmen claim that they overcommitted themselves in reaction to the riots, out of a desire to purge themselves of a sense of guilt and responsibility, but also to placate the many forces in government and community groups that were pressing for action. Four factors explain the present tendency toward reflection rather than more activity.

1. After the relatively "cool" summers of 1968 and 1969, public and governmental pressure on corporations to help relieve the urban crisis diminished. Board chairmen whose participation was actively solicited by high officials in the Johnson Administration say that pressure to act has not been as strong from the Nixon Administration. Even the intensity of appeals from nongovernmental groups, such as the National Urban Coalition and the National Alliance of Businessmen, seemed to diminish. Other issues—such as campus unrest—captured the attention of the public, and the news media assigned less prominence than before to outbreaks of urban disorder.

2. Corporate executives learned that urban affairs programs are much more costly than they ever anticipated. Some companies that declined opportunities for government aid for training programs now say they will have to have subsidies in order to continue their projects. Costs were higher than personnel officers expected, and top managers felt pressure from their own line officers to hold back on commitments unless broader budgetary allocations for training could be authorized.

3. Businessmen learned that the tasks of planning and managing urban affairs programs require more thought and skill than they realized. Somewhat humbled by experience, they are now reluctant to set their hopes too high for future achievement. "We really didn't know what we were getting into," said one chief execu-

tive officer. "We were pressed hard to act fast, and unfortunately we did." Many executives admonish themselves for learning too late that the skills required for managing urban affairs programs are not the same as those needed to run a successful business.

Some observed that urban affairs activities threaten the financial interests of their shareholders.

4. Urban affairs programs have had unanticipated, sometimes unwelcome, effects on the internal life of large companies. In some cases, these effects go far beyond dollar costs. For example, when a new program calls for the hiring of large numbers of disadvantaged blacks, managers have to cope with objections and resentment expressed by old-time employees. Often these side effects were not anticipated and led to production delays as well as intergroup tensions. Managers of companies so affected say that a transition period is needed while they learn to cope with these new problems.

On the whole, few companies are satisfied with the progress they have made. To be sure, the evidence suggests that most of them reacted with more energy than discretion to government pleas for urban affairs programs. Some of the most resourceful and powerful companies in the country encountered difficulties. Though no one said he wanted to give up, responses from a large majority of the executives interviewed revealed general disappointment that so little had been accomplished.

THE URBAN AFFAIRS PROGRAM PATTERN

Formally organized urban affairs programs are a relatively new development in the corporate world. Though 201 of the 247 companies in the study now have some sort of urban affairs program under way, only four of these were set up before 1965.

Urban affairs programs were classified into five categories for the purpose of the study. The program pattern, the numbers of companies active in each category, and the percentages for each type of involvement are shown in Table 1. Variation by industry

Table 1. The Urban Affairs Program Pattern

Category	Number of Companies	Percentage
Donations of cash, staff, executive time, and/or facilities	175	70
Minority group hiring programs	110	44
Hard-core hiring programs	86	34
Hard-core training and upgrading programs	39	16
Other urban affairs activities	30	12

with respect to type and degree of urban affairs involvement is, of course, to be expected. While certain industries tend to lead in certain types of programs, banks, utilities, insurance, and aerospace companies are in the vanguard in all or most of the categories. (See Table 2 for comparisons.)

THE MOTIVES BEHIND THE PROGRAMS

Enlightened self-interest. After conscience, the principal motive offered by top executives in the 201 companies with urban affairs programs is enlightened self-interest. Virtually all the companies interviewed insisted that their sense of social responsibility impelled them toward action after Watts, Detroit, and Newark. "Our urban affairs work is good for Chase Manhattan in a strictly business sense," said David Rockefeller. "Our efforts are aimed at creating a healthy economic and social environment that is vital to the existence of any corporation." This theme was repeated many times. James F. Oates, Jr., chairman of the board and chief executive officer of the Equitable Life Assurance Society, indicated that "As businessmen, our responsibility in serving social change is great. Our responsibility to serve it well is even greater."[1] Most respondents pointed out that business depends for its continued existence on the availability of skilled manpower and also on conditions of social stability. Therefore, they felt that it was only common sense to try to solve social problems that could threaten their future.

[1] James F. Oates, Jr., *Business and Social Change* (New York: McGraw-Hill Book Company, 1968), p. 68.

4

Table 2. Extent of Corporate Involvement in Urban Affairs, 1967-70

Industry	Number of Companies						
	Surveyed	Contributing Cash, Executive and Staff Time, and Facilities	Employing Minority-Group Members	Hiring Hard-Core Unemployed	Training Hard-Core Group	Sponsoring Other Urban Affairs Programs	Percent Participating in All Five Programs
Banks	14	14	9	7	5	11	66
Office machinery and computers	6	3	5	4	3	4	63
Motor vehicles	8	3	8	6	4	3	60
Aircraft and aerospace	15	8	12	11	5	8	59
Insurance	39	28	32	20	12	16	55
Scientific and photographic equipment	6	3	5	4	2	2	53
Utilities	11	9	7	6	3	3	51
Electronics and appliances	20	14	10	10	5	11	50
Merchandising	15	12	10	4	0	5	42
Petroleum	30	15	15	4	2	8	29
Transportation	9	4	6	1	1	0	27
Food and beverage	18	11	7	5	0	0	26
Building materials	13	4	4	2	0	2	19
Farm and industrial machinery	8	2	3	1	0	0	15
Chemicals	13	5	4	0	0	0	14
Metal manufacturing	8	3	2	0	0	0	13
Other	14	7	9	5	2	6	41
Total	247	145	148	90	44	79	41

Appearance. For four-fifths of the companies interviewed, strengthening corporate reputation and image is a key objective of urban affairs efforts. Now that student and organized consumer groups as well as shareholders have begun to investigate the effect of corporate activities on public problems, urban affairs programs are seen by corporate officials as one way to pacify, satisfy, or even silence their critics.

Many companies, of course, invest their urban affairs budgets mainly in "public information" programs. They publish material dramatizing or exaggerating their service activities; their annual reports describe even minor urban affairs efforts in great detail. Special brochures are used to publicize programs. Several years ago, AT&T began publishing a monthly magazine beating the drum for its urban affairs efforts, particularly its recruitment and training for blacks. The Chase Manhattan Bank in New York publishes "Action Reports" to describe its efforts, as well as several bulletins and newsletters.

"Many companies," according to Whitney Young, Jr., "limit their concern to press releases, empty speeches, or less. I remember listening," he said, "to the head of a major corporation brag about all his firm was doing. After some close questioning, I found the sum total of these grand efforts added up to less than two dozen summer jobs for black youths in only 3 of the 60 cities in which that company operates."[2]

Compliance. Two-fifths of the companies interviewed adopted their programs in order to meet government equal opportunity requirements in employment and in the awarding of contracts. One executive said, "Our policy against discrimination was arrived at in response to the law—not conscience, civic spirit, or sentiment." Another said, "We are not in the charity or social welfare business. We do only what we have to do to maintain profitability."

Insurance. One-third of the companies studied hoped that their programs would help discourage boycotts, violence, and other threats to company well-being. As one manager put it, "The last

[2] Quoted in the *New York Times*, January 11, 1970.

6

thing we need is a summer work-in by SDS." Ralph Nader's Project for Corporate Responsibility is the type of consumer effort that has caused anxiety among corporate executives. And Nader's questions about the impact of certain corporate policies on public problems probably represent only the beginning of concerted drives to make big business accountable to consumer interests. Some companies recently forced to justify their reputations for community service are American Telephone and Telegraph Co., General Electric, Honeywell, Gulf Oil, Union Carbide, The Columbia Broadcasting System Inc., Eastman Kodak, and Pepsico Inc.

Profit. One-eighth of the companies interviewed were frank about their interest in opening up new markets by attracting black customers, or by selling their services, perhaps as trainers or consultants, for urban affairs projects. "Urban affairs is a new market for us," said one executive. "Because of the poverty program, we bagged some government contracts for the first time." James Kalish, a free-lance management consultant, has written about the birth of a new industry geared toward the exploitation of urban problems for private profit. Kalish is probably right that this new industry is mainly "flimflam, double-talk and hustle."[3]

The reader should not conclude that the forty-six companies in the sample that have no urban affairs programs are either unmoved by the foregoing factors or oppose urban affairs activities on principle. Most of these companies claimed that they simply could not afford urban affairs efforts at present. Only five acknowledged that they are not interested in urban programs. Thus, the executive vice-president of one company explained that he and his staff only have time for activities that will improve corporate earnings. "We serve our social function by striving to increase per share earnings," he said. Another of the company's officers declared, "In our type of business we don't have to worry about the minority group market. We sell our services to affluent professionals—engineers, doctors, and chemists." Few claimed that the only business of business is business.

[3] James A. Kalish, "The Urban Affairs Problems Industry," *Washington Monthly*, November 1969, pp. 58–68.

RANGE OF ACTIVITIES

The most prevalent corporate urban affairs programs are: (1) donations; (2) minority employment and advancement; (3) hiring and training the disadvantaged; and (4) assistance to community economic development, black capitalism, and environmental improvement efforts. In the chapters that follow, the progress and achievements of each of these programs are discussed in detail, and analyses of key issues and prospects for the future are also provided.

2

Corporate Donations Programs

Corporate acts of community service traditionally have taken the form of financial contributions to nonprofit groups and institutions rather than direct service through programs and projects. The list of community activities financially aided by big business but implemented by others has been continually expanding, and includes projects in health, child care, education, recreation, civil rights, air and water pollution control, voter information, narcotics control, and treatment of alcoholism.

The benevolent instincts of board chairmen and company directors are, of course, encouraged and even engendered by the Internal Revenue Code. Yet corporate giving, despite its enormous potential, has been a relatively small part of total national giving. In a recent study of corporate philanthropy for education, Patrick and Eells[1] pointed out that while total business contributions in dollars multiplied roughly twenty-seven times between the late 1930s and the late 1960s, it decreased as a total of national philanthropy from 6.15 percent in 1950 to 6 percent in 1966.

[1] Kenneth G. Patrick and Richard Eells, *Education and the Business Dollar* (New York: The Macmillan Company, 1969), p. 6.

Business giving for all causes from 1936 to 1939 averaged $30 million a year. In 1950, it amounted to $252 million; in 1956, $418 million; in 1960, $482 million.[2] In each of these years, business contributions represented 0.1 percent of gross national product and slightly more than 0.1 percent of personal income, and they increased little as a percentage of net profit before taxes— from 0.59 percent in 1950 to 1 percent in 1966.[3]

The following report on business donations to urban affairs projects must be viewed in the perspective provided by the above figures. No matter how benevolent some big companies have been, corporate philanthropy as a whole has been meager in relation not only to corporate profits, but also to other private philanthropy.

Historically, most corporate philanthropy was carried out to suit the personal inclinations of top executives. It was managed in an unsystematic, uncoordinated way, unlike other aspects of business performance. The guidelines that govern other corporate activities were seldom observed. Today, too, most company donations programs fail to identify objectives, select and develop effective strategies for achieving them, or apply measures of desired performance. Recipients of funds tend to be chosen on the basis of personal, intuitive criteria. This study's findings show that in most major companies, the review of requests for funds is conducted by executives who carry other corporate responsibilities. Sometimes board chairmen and presidents attend to donations policies, on an *ad hoc* basis, a few times a year. Responsibility for screening applicants or developing projects is seldom placed in the hands of a professional staff.

Causes catching the fancy of, or reflecting the values, creeds, or affiliations of, corporate directors and chairmen tend to be most frequently favored with bestowals from corporate coffers. Not surprisingly, business has supported mainly the older, hallowed welfare organizations, those legitimated by custom and by a conservative approach to social work. The Salvation Army, the Red Cross, the Community Chest/United Fund (now known as the United

[2] *Ibid.*, p. 5.
[3] *Ibid.*

Way), and other nationally organized charities traditionally received the largest corporate contributions, along with the Boy Scouts, Girl Scouts, settlement houses, and similar noncontroversial groups. Until recently, urban affairs causes as such were seldom singled out by corporate donors, and when they were, they were given no higher priority when money was being doled out than the president's alma mater or his wife's parents' parish.

CHANGING PATTERNS OF BUSINESS GIVING

Beginning in 1967, a new or heightened sensitivity to urban problems on the part of business executives led to changes in patterns and styles of corporate donations policies. Of the 247 companies in the study sample, 175 revised their annual donations lists after 1967 to provide for grants to groups identified specifically with urban problems. (At the same time, 45 of these companies actually reduced their donations to traditional charities.) Amounts annually given to urban affairs activities since 1967 by individual companies ranged from $10,000 to in one case, $750,000. The average figure was close to $175,000.

Some companies set aside donations money for the urban crisis after the riots in Watts, Detroit, and other cities, earmarking funds for support of urban affairs activities and organizations. Contributions then flowed into the treasuries of the National Urban Coalition or local Urban Coalitions, which, because they list prominent industry leaders as sponsors and board members, seem to assure donors that their money would be spent just as respectably and patriotically as it had been by, for example, the Girl Scouts.

Other organizations benefiting most from the heightened awareness of city problems by corporate donors are the National Alliance of Businessmen (NAB) and those oriented to the needs of black Americans: the National Association for the Advancement of Colored People, the Urban League, and the United Negro College Fund.

The data show that one-fourth of the 247 companies have added at least one of the latter three groups to their donations lists since

1967; another 23 companies, that contributed to these organizations before 1967, reported that they are now giving larger amounts. "We used to make a token contribution to the NAACP," said a company treasurer in a midwestern city. "Since 1968 it has received our largest grant."

Local community organizations have also begun to benefit from the change in corporate donations policies. Nearly one-fifth of the companies studied donate funds for grass-roots "selp-help" programs, neighborhood improvement projects, community education programs, and other locally organized and operated projects. Neighborhood and community group leaders, who probably would have been turned away by receptionists in executive suites five years ago, today receive the kid-glove treatment, and are frequently invited into the president's office for handshakes and picture-taking, even when donations are not forthcoming.

"After the Watts riots, we realized we needed to open diplomatic relations with neighborhood leaders to win their confidence and friendship," said a chief executive in San Francisco. "We started by setting up a series of meetings in slum neighborhoods. I think our efforts saved us from the angry demonstrations organized against a few of our competitors." Twenty-seven companies did not wait to be approached; they went out and looked for new urban causes and groups to befriend. A community leader in Watts told about a phone call he received from the public relations officer of an aerospace company: "He wanted to know if we would accept a contribution. Would you believe that the mountains are coming to Mohammed these days?"

Thirty-six of the companies in the study reported that they provide scholarship funds for programs in urban affairs through their own foundations. One company supports a college scholarship program for slum residents in Pittsburgh. Another provides funds earmarked for graduate fellowships for blacks. Funds of other company-owned foundations are deposited in black-owned banks and loaned at below-the-market interest rates to qualified community groups and welfare organizations. Other activities include sponsorship of community information projects and arts projects in slum neighborhoods.

The corporate conscience has not responded enthusiastically to demands of the militant minority group organizations, such as CORE, SNCC, or the National Welfare Rights Organization. Twenty-seven of the companies interviewed had been approached by representatives of these groups, but only three—an automobile maker, a computer manufacturer, and a nationwide chain of retail stores—responded with cash donations. Big business patrons are inclined, when they give money to blacks, to stay in the middle of the road.

Nor is the conscience of the corporations particularly moved by requests from fund-raisers for white minority group organizations. Charities for ethnic interest groups were seldom mentioned by interviewees; those that did receive money obtained relatively small grants. White ethnic groups have less bargaining power than black groups with corporate donors who are eager to respond to urban pressures. Right or wrong, they are seen as less deserving—at least for now. Whether big business givers will be hit by an ethnic backlash as white minority group organizations press for equal support remains to be seen.

Some companies choose donations as their major urban affairs effort. They would rather express corporate conscience in cash than in the time or the patience and tolerance required by employment-oriented programs. In addition, their executives do not enjoy the prospect of participating in community meetings. John Gardner referred to this standoffishness of businessmen when he said, "We could get a lot more action if we told them they didn't have to sit down at a table with anyone but could just . . . raise the money and then lob it over the walls of the ghetto."[4] Some of the top executives with whom I talked confirmed Gardner's observation. They admitted that they would rather make generous donations than have to attend meetings with community leaders, whether friendly or hostile.

[4] *Business and Society*, vol. 2, no. 8 (October 1969), p. 6.

Some companies have a different reason for preferring cash donations. They do not want to confront organizational changes required when programs for unskilled, disadvantaged employees are introduced. The need to set up a new department or rewrite the rules governing day-to-day behavior of personnel irritates and worries executives in these companies more than the dollar cost of donations.

When they select the donations route, managers can avoid anxiety about the by-products of special hiring programs—new training requirements, new approaches to hearing and adjudicating grievances, new rules and standards governing employee behavior, and the possibility of intergroup tensions in the plant or office.

These companies feel so strongly about their preference for cash donations as opposed to entanglement in urban action programs that their donations programs sometimes are budgeted for as much or more than urban affairs manpower training efforts, for example, in other companies. One wonders, however, whether they will always be able to avoid setting up special programs. The question is how long organizations of blacks will be willing to accept cash instead of action programs.

Effects on Older Charities

Changing tastes in corporate philanthropy in response to pressures from newer urban affairs groups has led leaders of some older groups to reappraise their activities and reshape programs. Writers of grant proposals, developers of program ideas, the guardians of and lobbyists for older, established groups, who formerly could count on continuing support from corporate patrons, have felt the impact of the shift in corporate giving patterns. Intentionally or not, big business has helped update the policies and interests of settlement houses, voluntary welfare agencies, and nationally organized fund-raising groups. These groups have always sought to stay abreast of the preferences of those who award government and foundation grants. Similarly, they need to be sensitive to the wishes of donors in the business world.

14

We used to be "the fair-haired boys of business leadership," said William Aramony, executive vice-president of the United Community Funds and Councils of America (the United Way). "They were interested in eliminating the major part of the multiple fund-raising nuisance, and we did that job reasonably well." But funding sources are increasingly interested in the content of programs and their credibility with client groups, before awarding money. "They . . . insist on programs that work," Aramony said, "that affect people's lives meaningfully so that tensions are reduced and order is possible." He warned that his and similar organizations could lose the support of big business unless they revised their programs to satisfy the new criteria demanded by business.[5]

Many of the urban affairs officers (whose jobs are new in the corporate world) are also pressuring for changed donations policies. "I didn't like to see our foundation's money being doled out to the same bland do-good groups," said the urban affairs manager of an aerospace company in Los Angeles. "Our president was persuaded by my argument, and flatly told the local charity leaders that they would have to involve themselves in neighborhood projects in order to continue to receive our support." To compete with the newer groups, older welfare agencies have had to reformulate their strategies in order to attract corporate money.

At a recent meeting of the American Management Association in New York City, a vice-president of a large insurance company near Philadelphia, who is black, reported that he had successfully appealed to his company's president to order a reappraisal of donations policies. "I knew we had given money each year for two decades to the do-good local charities, the kind that didn't even need us because they were popular with everyone else. I compiled a list of alternate possibilities for gift-giving—smaller, but new, indigenous, and struggling organizations. We began to channel some of our money into the bank accounts of these smaller groups."

To be sure, some business givers have leaned the other way and withheld grants from groups identified with causes they consider

[5] *New York Times*, April 11, 1970.

to be too militant, or unfriendly to corporate interests. The refusal to give is a potent weapon, too. University fund-raisers cite examples of companies that reduced or cancelled their annual donations as a way of registering disapproval of student protesters. A front page editorial in *Barrons*, the national financial weekly, urged businessmen not to subsidize the enemy: "The cadres marching on American business have trained at Berkeley, Wisconsin, Cornell and hundreds of other schools. The propaganda which has set them in motion has been going on a lot longer. Isn't it incredible that American businessmen and financiers are still so naïve as to think they are being charitable when they support institutions and individuals who, measure by measure, move us all closer to the end of the capitalist system?"[6]

Risks for the Donor

Despite the new pattern of donations, few companies have made efforts to identify and evaluate the many new, community-based self-help groups or other rapidly proliferating urban affairs efforts. Board chairmen who could rely at one time on personal acquaintanceships with the leaders of charities soliciting their aid, or on lifelong familiarity with the work of established groups, are not likely to have rubbed elbows with black militants or to have a sense of who's who in the ghetto community. Executives in charge of corporate donation programs are aware of the high price charged for ignorance or naiveté when it comes to choosing among the many groups seeking company donations. Many of these executives have seen or heard about damaging political repercussions that resulted from unwise decisions about grants. "We have been boycotted by groups on both sides of a major issue in this city because we gave money to all of them," said the president of a large western paper products company. "Either we're too radical or too 'redneck.' " "We receive scores of requests for money daily," said

[6] *Barrons National Business & Financial Weekly*, May 18, 1970.

one company spokesman. "And frankly we don't know how to choose."

Companies that updated their donations policies sometimes find themselves the target of criticism from shareholders and customers. Thus, community groups are not the only source of protest worrying corporate donors. "I doubt that any of our shareholders has sold his stock because we gave to the Urban League, but I won't be surprised when it happens," said one top executive. The consequences of denying requests for assistance have to be weighed very carefully. "You can't play it safe by not giving, either," said another officer. "A lot of the younger people on our staff have been telling us to put our money where our mouth is," said the president of a large Chicago-based company. "So we are planning to announce a large contribution for a slum improvement project later this month."

The choice between the familiar, safe, do-good groups and the controversial, less safe, but sometimes more effective and more vocal groups is a difficult one to make. Experience and political sophistication, as well as a dash of courage, are needed by the corporate patron who wants to discover and lend a hand to some of the newer groups. Unfortunately, corporate donation policies have tended to be a means of massaging the president's conscience, or satisfying the tax accountant's goals of providing expense write-offs. But donations programs could be administered to achieve more positive goals, and business patrons could be encouraged to give in order to have optimum effect on community programs. Because every dollar donated is eventually charged at least partly against corporate income, managers might just as well measure themselves rigorously with regard to donations and aim to get good performance for their dollars. What is needed in every company is a clear definition of performance objectives for donations policies.

The study showed that few attempts have been made on the part of corporations systematically to identify, evaluate, and select from all possible agencies, groups, and causes in the urban arena. Clearly there are opportunities to give that have not yet been explored;

there are groups that have not yet caught the eye of corporate officers.

The majority of the executives interviewed reported that their companies maintain foundations for the express purpose of giving money away but that these foundations concentrate on receiving rather than seeking applications. Most applications for financial assistance are unsolicited. And most foundation officers reported that more than half of the total number of groups that ask for money receive it. "If they know us well enough to ask us for money, we generally know them well enough to give it to them."

Accountability

Many aspects of corporate donations programs call for exploration and study. Through gift-giving, corporations are able to influence social policy, the destinies of private programs, and the success of community groups. Corporate urban affairs achievements would receive a significant boost if all the corporations donating money to the Boy Scouts or to the alma maters of their board chairmen were to divert a percentage of these contributions to neighborhood groups, economic development projects, or manpower training programs.

But corporate conscience is not the only motive behind corporate philanthropy. Sometimes the givers do not choose to achieve anything more than ingratiating themselves with recipients, or pacifying a pressuring public. A corporate gift can be a bribe, paid in return for a gadfly group's promise to keep still and refrain from criticism of corporate policies. Just as a mayor will grease the wheel that squeaks, so will a corporation president.

Critics of the big corporations, including Ralph Nader, have not yet turned their attention to corporate donations policies. Nor did congressional investigations of the large foundations focus on corporate philanthropy. A study of the techniques, management, and decision-making processes of big business donors, would provide useful information for students of corporate urban affairs efforts, as well as for the donors themselves.

Congressman Wright Patman's discoveries about the criteria used in gift-giving by family-held foundations suggests the potential value of a similar inquiry into the practices of company-owned foundations. Speaking mainly of the large, private, and family-controlled foundations, he charged that they "appear to be afflicted with charitable myopia, if not outright blindness."[7] Thus he pointed out, "while Puerto Rican children in Harlem fell behind in their studies because of language problems, the Lilly Endowment, Inc., of Indianapolis, sent $15,000 [to a university in] Mexico City . . . and a Rockefeller-controlled foundation . . . sent $311,280 to [an English-language program in] Tokyo." Similarly, "while our central cities fell into decay and Negro youths rioted in our streets, the Bollingen Foundation (a Mellon family foundation in New York City) sent thousands of dollars abroad to uncover the dust of centuries and study 'Roman and Etruscan town plans.' "[8] But what of expenditures by foundations set up by the large banks and petroleum, insurance, and pharmaceutical companies? To which groups do these companies donate money? Whom do they turn down? What standards do they employ in making awards?

If the allowance of deductions from taxable income is to be continued, then surely corporate foundations should be required to make their objectives, goals, and operating procedures, as well as their expenditures, fully visible. Criteria used by all foundations in evaluating requests should be available for public scrutiny. Even further, companies could be encouraged to reach out to find and help groups conducting useful urban affairs programs. To accomplish this latter goal, business needs to improve its fact-finding abilities about donations possibilities.

CORPORATE VOLUNTEERS

In addition to funds, roughly one company in four reported donating staff and facilities as part of its urban affairs efforts. Ad-

[7] U.S., Congress, House., Select Committee on Small Business, Subcommittee Chairman's Report, *Tax-Exempt Foundations and Charitable Trusts*, 90th Cong., 2nd Sess., March 26, 1968, p. 2.
[8] *Ibid.*

vice on financial management, general administration, public relations, and manpower training are offered free of charge by corporate experts, not only to large urban affairs organizations, but to neighborhood groups as well. In New York, for example, the Chase Manhattan Bank estimated that several hundred employees volunteered time in a two-year period to assist community projects in disadvantaged neighborhoods. Typically, companies report that they have one or more executives serving on a community board, working with the Urban Coalition, advising an antipoverty council or a Model Cities project, or on loan to the National Alliance of Businessmen. However, while nearly 40 percent of the 247 companies in the study encouraged staff members to help out on community projects, *less than half of these let them do so on company time.*

Corporate officials help black businessmen with their management problems; others assist educators in improving school programs, lead youth groups in slum neighborhoods, and provide coaching on job-hunting techniques. Staff specialists offer advice about financial management to a wide variety of public and private urban affairs groups. For example, Western Electric set up a company-wide service project in New Jersey, under which employees volunteer for work in social agencies or with youth groups. Employees serve after hours and on weekends in neighborhood renewal work and in a street academy program.

In addition to contributions of funds and staff time, corporations have donated facilities and equipment to neighborhood groups in many cities. The Green Power Foundation in Los Angeles, a business conglomerate formed by local leaders, received gifts of heavy manufacturing and food-processing equipment, and packaging materials.

In a survey conducted in 1969 by the American Bankers Association, members were asked to estimate the total hours of management time contributed to private and public organizations and the value of his contribution in dollars. In hours per month, the range was from 200 to 2,100. In dollars, the contribution was estimated at as much as $20,000 per month by one large metropolitan bank.

Through donations of staff time, corporations can influence the decisions of such groups as the Urban Coalition, as well as indigenous community groups. Thus, in New York and other major cities, the local Urban Coalition boards include representatives of major banks and insurance companies. Staff members are granted leaves of absence with pay for service in such organizations. The Chase Manhattan Bank in New York assigned two officers to the Coalition from its public relations department, for one-year tours of duty. Even when he cannot influence policy, the volunteer businessman often has the opportunity to neutralize what might otherwise be an antagonistic or hostile board, or at least to keep his company informed of activity in the grass roots.

3

Removing Barriers For Minority Groups

The rhetoric of the urban crisis has focused on the problems of only some minority groups; it has neglected others. Thus big business's urban affairs employment efforts are designed to provide jobs and training for blacks, with special attention given to the disadvantaged and the young. The need to provide job and training opportunities for other minority group members receives scant attention from personnel directors. Their lack of interest is encouraged by government manpower policy, which stresses the needs of disadvantaged blacks. No subsidies are offered for training or upgrading low-income members of white minorities, the lower middle class, or even some working class members.

To be sure, industry attempts to satisfy equal employment opportunity requirements of federal, state, and local laws. But none of the companies interviewed said they were conducting programs to recruit, train, or upgrade nonblack minority group members. The federally sponsored JOBS program can serve as a convenient escape hatch for companies who want to demonstrate that they abide by equal employment opportunity regulations. Hiring the disadvantaged and receiving subsidies for their training has become a means for avoiding the hiring of other minority group members.

23

Special programs for the disadvantaged, writes Michael J. Piore, "may be a *substitute* for nondiscrimination in normal procedures. It may thus become much easier for a black to be hired if he is disadvantaged than if he is not; or, more likely, the hiring of blacks may be channeled through special programs."[1]

This chapter begins a two-part discussion of urban affairs employment programs in industry. It focuses on the problems of ethnic and racial minorities, those whose only handicaps, from the perspective of corporate employers who oversee selection or promotion, are color, ethnicity, or religion. Some issues related to the status in large companies of Jews, Italians, Irish, blacks, and Spanish-speaking minorities are discussed here. Programs for the disadvantaged are described in Chapter 4.

Many ethnic minority group members work in blue collar jobs, but others are in white collar and management positions. Yet many members of these groups feel neglected by industry and are concerned by intensified efforts to serve the needs of the disadvantaged. After three years of corporate urban affairs programs for blacks, notice is only beginning to be taken of the alienation felt by some lower middle class ethnic groups. This alienation is seen by some as a grave threat to social stability. "The current ethnic disaffection on the racial issue, and the proven ability of neo-reactionary forces to capitalize on this disaffection, should be seen as a deep threat to America. The fall-out from racial conflict is converting many lower middle class Americans to a status quo posture on other issues, a posture that may not be in keeping with their economic position or their own self-interest."[2]

Since 1967, 110 of the 247 companies studied set up special outreach programs to recruit blacks for entry-level jobs. Most of the rest say that though they did not undertake formal programs, they stepped up their efforts to increase the number of black em-

[1] Michael J. Piore, "Discussion," *Programs to Employ the Disadvantaged*, ed. Peter B. Doeringer (Englewood Cliffs, N.J.: Prentice-Hall, 1969).

[2] Irving M. Levine, "A Strategy for White Ethnic America," A paper presented at the Philadelphia Conference on the Problems of White Ethnic America, June 1968 (New York: American Jewish Committee, 1968), p. 1.

ployees. On the other hand, only 9 percent of the companies in the study indicated that they had undertaken formal efforts in their communities leading to the recruitment or upgrading of white minority group members, such as Jewish, Irish, and Italian workers. Few respondents pointed to formal programs, but three large companies said that they were aware of the problems of these other groups and attempting, in informal ways, to open up more jobs to them.

PRESSURES TO REMOVE BARRIERS TO EMPLOYMENT

Probably the strongest impulse behind recent corporate efforts to recruit minority group workers is provided by state and federal equal opportunity legislation. Corporate personnel directors have only recently become accustomed to examination of their recruitment practices by public human rights commissions. The threat of government sanctions or reputation-damaging hearings has moved many companies to action.

In addition to pressures imposed by law and bureaucratic inspections, the hiring habits of corporate managers have been subjected to scrutiny by a growing body of corporation watchers (student protesters, civil rights groups, the women's liberation movement, consumer associations, and religious and ethnic associations). Concern over urban problems has intensified public interest in corporate personnel practices, and probably for the first time in their history some of the country's largest companies are taking a fresh look at their own employment criteria to see whether perhaps unwittingly they serve to exclude minority group applicants.

Some personnel directors have begun to feel stronger pressures than those exerted by bureaucrats and politicians. *Ebony* magazine reported that at a construction site in Pittsburgh the manager of a large building construction company was hauled to the edge of a fifth-floor framework by a black militant representing skilled construction workers and told, "If you don't hire my men, I'm gonna drop you." Eleven blacks were quickly hired.[3] A stockholders'

[3] Quoted in *Time*, April 6, 1970.

meeting of North American Rockwell was interrupted in February 1970 by members of the Black Workers Association of the company, who charged that NAR's policies kept minority group workers out of white collar jobs.[4]

Labor shortages have also inspired corporate efforts to hire minority group members. As the labor supply tightened in some industries, color became unimportant. "We aren't trying to find more blacks; we're trying to find more help," said the personnel director of a West Coast company. His point was echoed by representatives of other companies, particularly those with plants located in or near cities whose ethnic and racial composition changed drastically in recent years. "We've always hired most of our people from right around here," said a factory manager in a major New Jersey city. "Twenty years ago there were few Negroes in the neighborhood, and we had practically an all-white payroll. Now the area is occupied mainly by blacks, and our labor force reflects the change."

PRACTICES ADVERSELY AFFECTING MINORITY GROUP PROSPECTS

Minority group members who aspire to jobs in large corporations, and some who are already employed and are ambitious for advancement, face barriers that have nothing to do with their ability. Four practices in corporate employment policies adversely affecting the prospects of skilled minority group members became apparent in this study: (1) favoritism toward youth; (2) emphasis on recruiting minority group members for entry-level jobs; (3) credential requirements; and (4) religious, ethnic, and sexual discrimination.

Favoritism Toward Youth

Nearly half of the 110 companies with special recruitment programs for blacks concentrate their efforts on hiring young people

[4] See *Urban Employment*, vol. I, no. 5 (March 5, 1970).

between the ages of eighteen and thirty to fill entry-level jobs. Only a handful of companies reported efforts on behalf of older recruits. Occasionally, companies in labor-intensive industries with large numbers of jobs for unskilled or semiskilled workers reported special programs for age groups over thirty. Those companies tend to be in banking and insurance, where normal turnover rates in operations-level jobs are high, and the need for people able and willing to perform routine clerical functions all day (or all night) is insatiable.

A variety of activities designed to recruit young blacks for entry-level jobs are conducted. Many are sponsored jointly with community agencies and schools. The largest number of programs for youthful recruits are run by companies whose manpower shortages are increasingly serious. In addition to banks and insurance companies, many telephone companies and utilities sponsor programs.

The findings suggest that, regardless of public pressure and government programs, young people, white or black, are more welcome than adults in most companies. Interviewees told me that the young are "easier to train," more "adaptable to the routines" of the office, and that they "get along better" with other employees. Yet no one said his company had conducted experiments to test the validity of these assertions. Moreover, explanations based on the allegedly greater adaptability of the young trainees seem spurious from companies where the young are assigned to roles that isolate them from other employees—in the mail room, operating office machinery, or in clerical jobs. Asked for the reason for isolating a group of young black males in the same unit in a large Chicago bank, a supervisor replied, "They only feel secure with one another."

Emphasis on Entry-Level Jobs

When urban affairs programs favor the young, a company need provide jobs only at the entry level, and *it* can avoid the challenge of providing opportunity for skilled workers or for candidates for management positions or the executive suite. Two-thirds of the executives interviewed said they would like to see more minority group executives in their companies; but only twelve companies in the survey sample claimed efforts to recruit minority group members for managerial and executive positions. Other companies, including Sears Roebuck, IBM, and Standard Oil (New Jersey), announced pledges to cooperate with efforts to recruit blacks for managerial positions.[5] No programs to recruit or develop managerial talent among members of white minority groups were reported.

The evidence is far from encouraging for the long-term prospects of entry-level jobs offered by urban affairs employment programs. The young man hired for a position on the lowest rung of a company's ladder often finds that management has allowed no way for him to improve his status and earning power. The barriers to higher rungs on the job ladder remain, even when racial or ethnic bias is eliminated in low-level jobs. Few companies provide upgrading opportunities for graduates of their own entry-level training programs, even though one of the major findings of the Kerner Report was that many rioters, though fully employed, felt locked into low-status, low-income, dead-end jobs.

Credentialism

Educational qualifications are barriers to employment for large numbers of people. Rigid reliance on educational and experience credentials might well amount to a new form of discrimination, one that will effectively bar minority group members from job opportunities. "Educational credentials have become the new property in America," according to Ivar Berg.[6] Their use as a screening device systematically assigns large numbers of people, especially the young, to a "social limbo."[7]

Children of the poor who depend for their education on central city schools are sometimes denied advancement opportunities be-

---

[5] *Business Week*, June 20, 1970, p. 34.

[6] See Ivar Berg, *Education and Jobs: The Great Training Robbery* (New York: Frederick A. Praeger, 1970).

[7] *Ibid.*, pp. 185–86.

cause they never received adequate training in school. S. M. Miller and Pamela Roby have suggested that, in order not to perpetuate the biases of credentialism, industry ought to provide more and more opportunities for training and mobility for low-level workers.[8]

Until now, according to Miller and Roby, education was seen as a full-time experience for the young, a period in which they acquire the skills on which to base their working lives. But work and education could be integrated to enable workers to improve their skills and earning power while employed. Education for factory or office workers need not end in school, and those who are inadequately served by public education systems could be given new chances to learn in industry. Only a handful of the companies studied expressed interest in accepting responsibility for providing educational opportunities broader than those directly related to production needs.

Most employers are still attempting to enforce job qualifications developed many years ago and never since reappraised. Government officials who review industry's upgrading programs tend to accept company definitions of qualifications required to do the job. But these stated qualifications do not necessarily reflect levels of education and training actually needed for effective performance. Berg's studies of 585 workers in a Mississippi textile manufacturing company showed that educational achievement was in fact often inversely related to performance.[9] Criteria for job qualifications, made sacred by time and tradition in some companies, are due for reassessment.

In many companies the job ladder for clerical workers and other office workers ends at a rung identified as the boundary between professional and nonprofessional jobs. Rigid hierarchies of role and status, enforced for generations, still prevail. Strict separations are enforced between occupations. In a group of New York publishing companies in my study, no possibility of mobility existed from messenger to secretary, from secretary to researcher, from editor

[8] S. M. Miller and Pamela Roby, *The Future of Inequality* (New York: Basic Books, 1970).

[9] Berg, *Education and Jobs*, p. 87.

to executive, or even from clerk to typist to secretary. Furthermore, within these hierarchies of role, advancement was obtainable only via "experience" on the job. Nonwhite employees were concentrated at low-level jobs requiring few educational credentials, and they complained that it was nearly impossible to move from one hierarchy to another. "How do you like your job?" a supply clerk was asked. "I wish they'd teach me how to do something else so I could get out of the supply room. But you need a diploma for every other job in this company."

Another aspect of credentialism that continues to deprive many able candidates of opportunity is the requirement of a "clean" or trouble-free personal record. The ex-convict, the former juvenile delinquent, and the one-time addict are automatically denied consideration by many companies. The new in-migrant unable to provide personal references is also frequently turned away.

Sar Levitan, Garth Mangum, and Robert Taggart have pointed out that the JOBS program stimulated participating firms to re-examine their personnel policies, and led many observers to see the "Questionable relevance of educational credentials to job performance."[10] However, my study's findings suggest that though more liberal interpretation of credential requirements has already benefited trainees hired for the JOBS program, these new interpretations seldom affect other job applicants, who are screened by employment interviewers applying the old company standards.

Whitney Young remarked on the irrationality and injustice of some forms of credentialism during a meeting of the American Association of Fund Raising Counsel in New York City. He described the Urban League's efforts to integrate whites into its own organization. At first, he said, "the young whites simply couldn't meet our standards—they couldn't speak the language of the ghetto, they didn't know what it was to be poor." As a result, the Urban League had to "lower [its] standards so that the Ph.D.s from Cornell and

---

[10] Sar A. Levitan, Garth L. Mangum, and Robert Taggart III, *Economic Opportunity in the Ghetto* (Baltimore: The Johns Hopkins Press, 1970), p. 38.

the editor of the *Yale Law Review*" could qualify for work. If the Urban League can do it, Young said, white institutions can, too.[11]

Religious, Ethnic, and Sexual Discrimination

Liberalized policies for nonwhite applicants have been extended somewhat to members of other minority groups seeking employment in industry. But by and large, "minority group members," when the phrase is used by corporate spokesmen, means blacks or people with Spanish surnames. The employment needs of white minority group members, those who are Jewish, Irish, or Italian, for example, receive little attention from managers. However, increasing numbers of these other minority group members are finding jobs in the corporate world, as a by-product of efforts to employ blacks. "Once the big petroleum companies began to hire blacks," said a staff member of the Urban Coalition in an eastern city, "they decided that they might just as well hire some Jews, too." According to a top executive in a large insurance company, "When we set up our program to recruit black managerial talent, we decided it was time we loosened up on our resistance to white minority groups too."

Many executives openly admitted that nondiscriminatory hiring programs were a departure from previous policy, albeit unwritten. "I admit that we have been guilty on this issue," said a director in the headquarters office of a large management consultant firm. "We used to be anti-Semitic. But that has changed. Now we not only hire Jews, but we don't hesitate to fire them, either." Said an executive in a large New York bank: "You can usually tell when a man was hired in this place by his last name. Thirty years ago we had a bias in favor of Germans and Swiss, even for the lowest level job. Then during the war we began to let the Irish in. By Korea we were employing Italians and Jews. Now we employ blacks and Puerto Ricans."

If ethnic and racial heterogeneity is slowly coming to middle- and lower level corporate jobs, the executive suite is only begin-

[11] Quoted in *Non-Profit Report*, vol. III, no. 1 (January 1970), p. 15.

ning to open its doors to Jews, other ethnics, and nonwhites. Citing a recent study of religious discrimination conducted by the American Jewish Committee, *Business Week* concluded that "if anyone is excluded from the executive suite because of his faith it is the Jew."[12] According to that study, fewer than 9 percent of the executives in major corporations in New York City are Jewish, though Jews make up 25 percent of New York's population and 50 percent of its college graduates. In Hartford, where 10 percent of the population is Jewish, only 1.2 percent of executives in the insurance industry are. The average is reported as even lower in the shipping, oil, railroad, chemical, and electronics industries. In Detroit, only two-thirds of 1 percent of the white collar jobs at the three major auto companies are said to be filled by Jews.[13]

According to the American Jewish Committee's findings, admission to the executive suite is dependent on favorable answers to such questions as "Is he our kind?" or "Will he fit in with the crowd at the country club?"[14] These questions assess what students of discrimination have called *nonability* factors—the social and personal characteristics of candidates.[15] The typical Jew, in the minds of managers, is notable for his business-relevant abilities. The shortcomings of Jews, according to these same managers, are principally in their lack of social credentials that some managers feel are necessary for an executive. "The typical Jew is deficient not in matters of ability, but in matters of nonability." Simply stated, in order to combat discrimination against Jews, corporations will have to cease judging candidates in nonability terms. Assuming the need for personnel of high ability, the sacrifice might readily justify itself.[16]

The gap between the ideal of equal opportunity and the practice of discrimination on the basis of religion is still significant. "The

---

[12] *Business Week*, January 24, 1970, p. 38.

[13] *Ibid.*

[14] *Ibid.*, p. 39.

[15] See Robert P. Quinn, *et al.*, *The Chosen Few* (Ann Arbor: University of Michigan Institute for Social Research, 1968).

[16] *Ibid.*, p. 47.

existence of the fruits of prejudice at the level of top management in many businesses suggests that our managers and executives either do not accept the ideal of equal opportunity for all or that matters are so complex that the ideal somehow does not come into consonance with practice."[17]

Only one of the 247 companies in the study reported any special programs to recruit or train women. Though there were many programs for minority group youths, on investigation all were revealed to be for males rather than females. When the women's liberation movement scrutinizes industry, its leaders will doubtless discover many opportunities not yet open to women.

POLARIZATION AND SCAPEGOATING

Sharply increased hiring of blacks has had negative consequences in some companies. Problems growing out of resentment and hostility on the part of older employees toward new black or Spanish-speaking workers are frequently reported. In some cases, valued senior employees were said to have left a company to protest favoritism shown to new black hires. Reports of backlash can, of course, serve as a convenient alibi for managers for their indifferent hiring efforts. "I wish we could do more," said one executive, "but those men in the plant are so reactionary that we haven't dared to try." Thus, in what appears to be plain old scapegoating, the men in the executive suite blame the men on the production line for the company's failure to act. Despite their eloquent protests, there is no reason to assume that corporate managers and officers are more humane and less bigoted than foremen and supervisors.

Some managers are genuinely concerned about the backlash problem and understand its causes. "We've learned to give our white employees the same breaks we offer to disadvantaged blacks," said one executive. "We had a backlash problem until we made it clear that *everyone* would benefit from the new urban affairs program."

[17] Lewis B. Ward, "The Ethnics of Executive Selection," *Harvard Business Review*, vol. 43, no. 2 (March-April 1965), p. 121.

Attempts to prevent cleavages dividing employee groups receive top priority in a few companies. But many of the executives interviewed agreed that more had to be done to encourage white employees to want to cooperate with special hiring and training projects. The National Alliance of Businessmen, like many of the private consulting firms that have burst into bloom around the urban problem, offers workshops, seminars, and sensitivity sessions for companies having these new kind of personnel problems. Whether workshops or sensitivity training alone will solve the problems of overworked and overstrained supervisors, and underappreciated foremen and co-workers, remains an open question. More likely, business will have to consider providing material incentives—awards for reducing turnover and developing new workers, or even bonuses or pay increases for the extra work.

The Cool Breeze of Cultural Variety

Minority group hiring programs have had surprising but nonetheless welcome consequences in some companies. Executives assigned to urban affairs functions, particularly those charged with training or supervising new nonwhite employees, say that urban affairs involvement has altered their organizations in unexpected but pleasant ways. Mores governing job performance and everyday behavior (dress, speech, and decorum) are being changed after years of rigidity. Where earlier newcomers to corporate life automatically submitted to company requirements covering day-to-day details, black employees, in particular, have successfully resisted the strong organizational ethic of conformity. Anecdotes for a new chapter in corporate sociology are being provided by blacks who, in an atmosphere that was formerly strictly white shirt and short haircut, come to work wearing dashikis and "Afros." And as Jews, Italians, and Irish join black and brown Americans, the Protestant white middle class that used to dominate the executive world finds itself, willingly or not, in a dialectic with other ethnic and racial styles and attitudes.

Some of the executives and employees in companies undergoing ethnic and racial transition consider not only the company but themselves beneficiaries of the changes wrought by urban affairs. "Urban affairs is fun," said a telephone company executive, "and we never had much of that around here. I was one of those obedient parochial school types hired by this company 15 years ago. I spent my first 10 years keeping my mouth shut. The atmosphere is much freer now. These newcomers have helped me learn how to swing a little bit in this up-tight environment."

Young workers as well as blacks are agents of change. The authority of management over nonwork-related matters is increasingly challenged by youths who want treatment as equals, not inferiors, by their bosses. "I'm not part of the machinery," said a young blue collar worker in a large plant in California. "If I can't have my dignity I don't want to work here." The *New York Times* quoted a union representative in a steel plant in Chicago describing the difference between older and younger workers: "Most of the older workers in my area are immigrants. They're somewhat afraid of authority. When a foreman pushes them around they take it. The young generation coming in now won't take it. They want to be asked to do something, not to be told to do it."[18]

In some ways, of course, the new black employee has more bargaining power on such personal matters as dress and behavior, if not on advancement. Right or wrong, personnel directors and other supervisors think twice before summarily discharging or reprimanding blacks. "I'll complain to the equal employment opportunity people" is a threat to which managers are quite sensitive nowadays. Whatever the reason, the black man's presence in normally conservative banks, insurance companies, and industrial settings is helping to change the atmosphere. Some companies see the change as a threat, but in others even top managers sometimes admit that they are enjoying the cool breeze of cultural variety.

[18] *New York Times*, June 1, 1970.

4

Programs for the Disadvantaged

Responding to imperatives in the Kerner Report and to appeals from federal, state, and local officials, many of the country's largest corporations agreed to undertake recruitment and training programs for the disadvantaged. Donations to charities, the traditional public service strategies of big business, would be supplemented (or replaced, in some companies) by a new approach: the direct and affirmative action of hiring people formerly considered unemployable.

By July 1, 1970 the National Alliance of Businessmen (NAB) reported that its member companies had already employed over 338,000 of the disadvantaged,[1] or nearly four-fifths of the total population of the "hard core" of the urban poor identified in the Kerner Report.[2] NAB's figures are, at best, estimates, and there is con-

[1] Reported in the *New York Times*, December 26, 1970.

[2] The stigmatizing term "hard core," referring to poor people who lack vocational skills and are additionally handicapped by emotional problems and factors of environment or sociology has given way to a new term, the "disadvantaged." Labor Department criteria define the hard core or disadvantaged as "poor persons who do not have suitable employment and who are either: (1) school dropouts; (2) under 23 years of age; (3) 45

37

siderable debate about the number of eligible candidates who have been hired and trained.[3] Corporate efforts are alternatively evaluated as triumphant, disastrous, or merely promising, depending on the evaluator's perspective, ideology, and data sources. Conflicting judgments are continually made by mayors, governors, legislators, the bureaucrats who report to them, and, of course, by businessmen and their public relations representatives.

On only one point is there general agreement: the problems that arise in hiring and training the disadvantaged are tough ones, and the objectives of corporate programs, as presently defined, are not easily realized. Though it is difficult to determine how many of the disadvantaged have actually been served by industry's programs—a quantitative measure—it is possible to analyze and assess the qualitative aspects of corporate programs. In the present study of 247 companies, data were gathered about enrollees in these programs and their experiences. The kind of training provided, costs entailed, problems encountered, and short-term successes of nearly one hundred programs were examined. This chapter reports on programs under way in a group of representative major corporations, and identifies factors influencing their success or failure. The nature of the training challenge and the advantages and disadvantages of respective program types are discussed from the standpoint both of

---

years of age or over; (4) handicapped; or (5) subject to special obstacles to employment." (The latter "obstacles" include those caused by racial discrimination.)

[3] NAB figures, which cover recruitment and training carried out through the publicly subsidized JOBS program, administered in cooperation with the Department of Labor, are derived from reports provided on a voluntary basis by participating companies. Because of the difficulty in verifying data on the number of hires, terminations, and retentions over measured periods, NAB's totals have to be treated as very broad estimates. Even if the figures are close to correct, the absence of statistical information about the characteristics of each new employee render it impossible to determine the extent to which the disadvantaged rather than merely the unemployed benefited from special programs. Nor is reliable information about the extent and scope of training programs available. But as others have pointed out, even if some of the reports of hirings are erroneous, "nothing is lost except the credibility of NAB." Levitan, Mangum, and Taggart, *Economic Opportunity*, p. 30.

the needs of trainees and the requirements of managers and supervisors. Comparative costs of subsidized and unsubsidized programs are also identified. Finally, some issues arising out of the growth of a new mythology and technology of vocational training and counseling are discussed.

PARTICIPATION BY INDUSTRY

Of the 247 major companies studied, nearly one-third reported programs for the disadvantaged. They said they had hired a total of 8,000 from this special group and, out of that number, two-fifths received training. But the majority of companies who hired the disadvantaged did so without offering special training.

Participation in programs varied by industry. Labor-intensive industries and those dependent on government favors and/or goodwill are at the head of the class. The greatest percentage of participants is found in aerospace companies, financial institutions (including banks, savings and loan companies, and insurance companies), and companies manufacturing electronic and computer equipment. Companies reporting meager or no efforts predominate in merchandising, metal manufacturing, petroleum, farm and industrial machinery, and chemicals. (See Table 2.)

Executives of companies without training programs offered a variety of explanations. "Don't compare us with aerospace or insurance," said the president of a new conglomerate, after acknowledging that his company had not undertaken any urban affairs projects. "The insurance companies have more cash than we do, and those in aerospace had to go out of their way to be good citizens simply to keep the government money flowing." The president of a large retail chain pointed out that "it wasn't until after the Detroit riots that the automobile makers got busy. If their factories were in East Cupcake, they wouldn't be so energetic."

Some corporate spokesmen say they would like to do more, but are handicapped by a lack of appropriate equipment, training staff, or by a shortage of space for training purposes. Others claim that their production schedules are too tight to be adapted to the needs of the disadvantaged, or that supervisors in their plants would not be able to cope with the special training requirements of programs for the disadvantaged. Or they protest that their manpower needs are specialized, offering no openings for the unskilled.

Many companies reported that their urban affairs contributions are made through donations programs, the assignment of staff members to community projects, or loans to minority group businessmen. "We decided to settle for spending more money in support of other people's urban affairs endeavors, rather than take on the headaches ourselves," said one executive. In his company, as well as in scores of others, cash outlays are viewed as more affordable than the stresses and strains that are assumed to accompany programs for the disadvantaged. New kinds of people in the company, new training methods, new attitudes in grievance procedures, and the need for new rules of behavior for employees are among the side effects feared by those who choose not to participate.

It cannot be denied that hiring and training the disadvantaged makes more sense for certain industries than others. A need for unskilled workers has, understandably, proved to be the best incentive. Some managers speculated that they probably would have invested in training the disadvantaged if the riots had never occurred and there had been no Kerner Report. "We were at a point where we would try anyone and anything to keep our shops going," said the personnel director of a large utility in Chicago. "Our former sources of manpower were drying up. You have to understand that prejudice wasn't functional in this company any more. Therefore, we didn't need to be forced to give this new category of job candidates a try."

The attention that has been focused on unemployed blacks in urban centers has inevitably aroused the interest of recruiters for companies desperate for candidates to fill lower level jobs. For these companies, hiring programs for the disadvantaged were set up not as a social service but as an attempt to maintain normal operations. Thus telephone companies in Newark, Chicago, New York, Cleveland, and San Francisco were among the first employers of the disadvantaged, as they sought to fill operator jobs on equipment in inner city stations, jobs no longer attractive to others in the labor market.

Companies undertaking programs for the disadvantaged face many challenges. The tremendous volume of literature from promoters and advocates of industry participation stresses the special needs of the new employees. But chief executives who embark on programs soon come to learn, too, that they need to train managers and supervisors, and that the economic requirements of the new programs can be a major obstacle. Financially sound training cost structures are hard to establish. And while training is underway, production quotas must be maintained. There are also organizational and morale costs to anticipate.

BUSINESS'S PRECONCEPTIONS

The kinds of programs created by industry, as well as the expectations of industry leaders, are influenced by assumptions about training needs in programs for the disadvantaged, assumptions written into the federally subsidized JOBS program, but also embodied in programs conducted by business without government support. By now there has developed a view of the black disadvantaged worker that is practically official, and it is accompanied by fixed notions about the kinds of training and treatment he or she will need. These preconceptions affect the costs, shape, and conduct of programs, as well as whether or not a company will be willing to undertake training at all.

The major dogma, propounded over and over again in the speeches and writings of most propagandists for programs for the disadvantaged and in the feature stories in the business press, is that the disadvantaged are profoundly different from the rest of us. They are said to come from a different culture, have a different view of the world, and have different work habits, expectations, and values. Because they are so different, potential employers are warned that jobs alone are not enough to solve the problems they present. And it is said that conventional job training, as it is typically offered in industrial settings, is not enough either. New approaches to training are held to be essential for program success.

Industry's efforts for the disadvantaged have been encouraged to emphasize training as an essential accompaniment to employment. Companies participating in JOBS, or influenced by it, have been led to bombard disadvantaged employees and their co-workers and supervisors with a plethora of training: for the newly hired employee, there must be specially designed vocational training to teach him requisite job skills. But to help him overcome his "cultural differences," he will need to receive "attitudinal training" or psychological counseling. Co-workers and supervisors are also said to need "orientation" in order to be prepared for the challenges presented by the disadvantaged, and sometimes psychological counseling as well.

Most of the above assumptions about training needs are unsubstantiated by research data or practical experience. They are derived instead from the ideas in the minds of government policy makers and academicians about poor people who are black. Whether or not they are realistic assumptions, they have already had the effect of deflecting policy from an emphasis on employment as an end in itself to an emphasis on the idea that jobs will have no value without training. Thus they have encouraged the development of a training technology within the private sector, one of the results of which has been the reorganization and expansion of personnel departments to make room for companies hiring the disadvantaged. These assumptions have contributed to the costs of employing the disadvantaged. It is true, of course, that they have created jobs and demand for trainers, counselors, psychologists, lecturers, and many breeds of consultants. Unfortunately, however, they have probably also discouraged many executives from hiring the disadvantaged.

The remainder of this chapter reviews and assesses the typology of corporate programs for the disadvantaged. Training is emphasized in varying degrees in each of the programs to be reviewed. The extent to which training is necessary, or is a regrettable deflection from the goal of providing employment, is an issue ripe for full investigation and research. What kind of training is needed? Do some types of training do more harm than good? What have been the consequences of attempts to require psychological counseling for the disadvantaged and of attempts to "adjust" them to the corporate world? And what have been the effects of the well-intended but potentially explosive "orientation" programs for supervisors and co-workers? Answers to some of these questions are suggested in the program analyses and descriptions that follow and in the case study in Chapter 7 of one company's training efforts.

TYPOLOGY OF CORPORATE PROGRAMS

Four basic program models are used in training the disadvantaged: (1) on the job; (2) in a vestibule setting; (3) in a subsidiary intended to be "spun off" to community groups; or (4) in a company-owned subsidiary. (See Table 3.)

On the Job

On-the-job training is the most frequently selected approach in the companies studies: in the thirty-nine companies offering training along with jobs, 80 percent of all new hires are enrolled in programs of this type. The economics suggest the reasons. The on-the-job approach does not require costly separate facilities or special training staffs. Companies can undertake training without having to change their ongoing production procedures.

This approach does not allow for auxiliary training or basic skills education. For the most part, the burden of providing for the needs of the new workers falls on line personnel. And the problems faced by line managers forced to train, coach, and guide new employees as they learn to adjust to the production environment are among the most serious in the on-the-job model. It is important in any vocational training program that the trainer feel some empathy for the trainee and some degree of enthusiasm for the train-

Table 3. Types of Hard-Core Training

Training Methods	Program Description	Program Requirements	Some Advantages	Some Disadvantages
On-the-job training	Recruiting the hard-core poor and assigning them to production jobs immediately	Line supervisors and foremen must train as well as supervise Entry-level jobs suitable for people with little work experience must be available	Fewer added costs than other programs Company gets benefit of new hands immediately	Strains and tensions between new and old workers may slow or disrupt production Double standard of evaluation and reward required for new/old employees Supervisors have burden of training
"Vestibule" training	Creating a halfway house to provide training before transferring workers to normal production jobs	Separate facilities must be provided with special staff	Hard-core workers join production process only after acquiring skills New employees can develop *esprit* before going into jobs	Added costs for facilities and staff Can be criticized for "quarantine" of new employees Learning takes place in an artificial environment

Training subsidiary	Creating a subsidiary company offering real work experience to hard-core employees	A new company must be incorporated and a management team designated Separate facilities are required	Parent company's main operations are not affected Parent can train potential managers as well as workers	Parent must be concerned with providing a market, and management and financial assistance in addition to training aids Commitment not easily revised or withdrawn once subsidiary is set up
Training "spin-off"	Creating a subsidiary that is designed to be spun-off to employees and/or community groups	Corporation must work with community groups to design and establish its subsidiary Company must work on day-to-day basis with community	Parent corporation has opportunity for close relationship with community Parent can plan for giving up overall responsibility	Community groups will need to be responded to on a continuing basis Community pressures may determine management decisions

ing role. But when his training assignment is added to his normal work load, and no compensating adjustments are offered to him, he frequently views the trainees as burdens and is not enthusiastic about helping them. The trainee can serve as his scapegoat, the target of a displaced grudge inspired by an insensitive management. Thus executives who want to establish on-the-job programs must heed this problem, and provide some incentives for supervisors. A foreman will not be led to do an adequate job merely by a rousing speech delivered by the company president. Nor is there evidence that he will be motivated by lectures about the social value of working with the poor.[4] With good reason, he will expect to be paid for the extra work and frequently longer hours that are asked of him. The corporate spokesman who promises that his company will participate in programs for the disadvantaged, however noble his intentions, must be sensitive to the problems of his foremen. Otherwise, he will do more harm—to racial and ethnic relations in his company, to his foremen and supervisors, and to the feelings of the disadvantaged, who will bear the brunt of the wrath of their supervisors—than good. To date only a few companies have come to see that material incentives are needed to avoid irritation among supervisors and to encourage their cooperation. Though extra compensation or lightened work loads are rarely provided, revised or relaxed production deadlines have been tried in some companies as a means of relieving pressures on supervisors and co-workers.

High turnover is a serious problem in companies with on-the-job programs. Vestibules and subsidiaries, described below, have much lower attrition rates than on-the-job programs. Employee retention rates in the latter averaged 30 percent in the companies studied; in the former, rates were 43 percent. There is even a difference in the way employees drop out of training. Those in on-the-job programs often just fail to return on Monday morning, leaving foremen to speculate about the reasons. On the other hand, dropouts from

[4] See Frank Riessman, "Jobs Are Not Enough for the Hard Core," Address before the American Society for Training and Development. Mimeographed; available from New Careers Center, New York University, New York.

vestibule or subsidiary programs behave differently, according to respondents. They tend to announce that they will be leaving or offer some clue about their intentions. Sickness, family problems, acceptance of another job are the most common explanations of voluntary resignations offered in all programs. It is probably true that enrollees in on-the-job programs are less apt to feel some responsibility toward the company, the supervisor, or the work unit than those in other types of programs. Thus they resign by drifting away, offering no explanations. In the more personal, supportive training environment of the vestibule and subsidiary, the worker will feel more of an incentive to explain his actions, believing that the company and its representatives care about him.

Even though specially designed vocational training is provided by fewer than half of the companies in the study, belief in its importance is growing. Very high turnover rates among the new hires, particularly in the first weeks on the job, have brought home the message: Adequate training is likely to cost less than high attrition caused by indifferent or no training.

How much time does on-the-job training take? It can range from an hour to several days of coaching, or to coaching throughout the employee's tenure. Sometimes it is offered by specially trained supervisors. Occasionally psychological counseling services and remedial education programs are also provided, with psychologists and teachers available during work and lunch hours. One of the automobile companies hired a team of psychologists, who claimed special knowledge of the problems of the disadvantaged. Members of the team were supposed to serve as peripatetic advisers, wandering along the assembly line, conferring with foremen, co-workers, and disadvantaged new employees on request. A pharmaceuticals company hired a remedial reading teacher to give instruction during lunch breaks. In both companies first priority was given to training the new employee to do his job. The other services were assigned the second priority.

A few companies offering on-the-job training try to help members of the regular work force prepare for the new employees. Lecture and seminar programs of many kinds are offered. Because they are generally prepared by an urban affairs staff and seldom by social scientists or, an equally attractive alternative, by disadvantaged people themselves, the quality and results of these programs are not impressive. In filmstrips, lectures, or seminars, a company's regular troops, or selections of them, are indoctrinated with messages meant to elicit cooperation with the new programs, but just as likely to provoke anxieties about the newcomers and antagonism toward them. Most of the material presented develops the idea that disadvantaged employees are profoundly different from the rest of us, and that their behavior will, at first at least, seem strange, even exotic. The differences are emphasized, and they are explained on the basis of culture or class. These orientation classes provide an unnnecessarily dramatic overture to the arrival in some companies of the disadvantaged.

The headquarters training department of a public utility company issues a packet of materials labeled "urban orientation," containing "problem-solving" exercises for supervisors of the disadvantaged:

Incident #2

A woman who reports to you has just requested 3 days off to have an abortion. Outline below what action you would take.

Incident #3

One of your employees reported to work this morning obviously affected by alcohol consumed before coming to work. He has been boisterous all morning, and during lunch period insulted a fellow employee who has reported the incident to you. Outline below the action you would take.

Incident #4

You have learned that an installer who reports to you is carrying his small tools home with him and, on his own time, working on installation jobs he started earlier. Outline below the action you would take.

Incident #5

You have recently added a disadvantaged person to your work team. There has been no open problem but you have heard there is a great deal of smoldering discontent among many of the other members of the work team. Acceptance of the new man is important, because, if he is to make the maximum contribution to the team, he must work closely

48

with other members of the work force. Outline what action you would take.

Incident #6

One of your newly hired employees' mode of dress is causing you real problems. He is doing satisfactory work but is having difficulty in relating to his fellow workers and the customers. The employee insists on wearing a beard and loud, weird-looking clothing. His manner of dress has caused several customers to request that he not be sent back on any future service calls. Indications are that this man could make a good employee if he would shave and dress in an acceptable manner. Outline what action you would take.

In my view, the above illustrations of corporate "urban orientation" materials are alarmist and sensational. They tend as much to provoke as to lessen prejudice. However, the company's trainers insisted in interviews that the exercises are valuable. Readers interested in seeing other examples of dogma and stereotype in corporate urban affairs orientation materials are referred to publications of the American Management Association and the National Industrial Conference Board. These groups distribute much material that is useful and informative. But, on the other hand, they have helped disseminate the notion that the behavior of the hard-core or disadvantaged worker will shock the sensibilities of allegedly well-adjusted, well-mannered, and properly motivated co-workers and supervisors.*

The automobile makers, who probably took on a larger share of the disadvantaged than any other industry in the period immediately following publication of the Kerner Report, at first provided no special training for the new employees.[5] They assigned most to

---

* See, for example, Lawrence A. Johnson, *Employing the Hard-Core Unemployed* (New York: American Management Association, 1969); and Allen R. Janger and Ruth G. Schaeffer, *Managing Programs to Employ the Disadvantaged* (New York: National Industrial Conference Board, 1970).

[5] Levitan, Mangum, and Taggart have suggested that the automobile companies were probably motivated to hire large numbers of the disadvantaged as much by a tightening labor market as by a "blossoming" of their social consciousness. For in the peak production periods of 1967–68, when demand for output was high and the available labor supply low, these companies had nowhere else to go for unskilled help. Levitan, Mangum, and Taggart, *Economic Opportunity*, p. 31.

49

their operations and assembly jobs, sometimes after only a few hours of orientation. But as turnover rates began to climb, they realized that intensive effort was needed. Other companies also intensified their training programs after a period of trial and error. When managers saw unusually high turnover rates, they set up specially designed orientation and counseling projects for new employees.

Vestibule

An isolated facility run by a special training staff, the vestibule is a halfway house, where the disadvantaged employee can adjust to "the world of work" by learning the habits and discipline expected during the workday, as well as the basic features of the jobs he will do.

The aim of the vestibule approach is to ease whatever anxieties the newly hired disadvantaged worker might have by providing him with the opportunity to practice his job before fully assuming the responsibilities necessary in a real production environment. He can acquire job skills with the coaching of foremen who are expected and paid to be sympathetic and patient with personal as well as work problems. In the vestibule, the foreman is concerned with the trainee rather than with production.

Despite the attractiveness of the vestibule as a training environment, only 18 of the 247 companies studied settled on this approach. Most of those who decided against the vestibule strategy were discouraged by the extra costs involved in obtaining and equipping the separate facility and in paying a separate training staff. Companies with vestibule programs argue that in the long run costs balance out, for they insist that attrition and turnover rates are significantly lower than in on-the-job programs.

The vestibule approach has several other attractions. By assuring that disadvantaged workers will take their places in normal operations only after they acquire basic skills, it minimizes the extent to which their arrival in the plant or office will provoke hostilities from on-the-line workers who might resent their effect on ongoing production processes. Because the special attention and dispensation sometimes required by disadvantaged workers can arouse antagonism on the part of other workers, isolating trainees during the period in which they need help most can avoid conflict.

The vestibule can protect trainees from seasonal layoffs that hit other parts of a company. Employees in the vestibule can be exempted from the company's seniority rules because they work in a special division. But this device does not always work. Thus, trainees in Chrysler's vestibule operations were laid off, along with other employees, when the company had to terminate its programs in March 1970, as the result of the downturn in the economy. (Chrysler cancelled its JOBS contract of $13.8 million providing hiring and training of 4,450 production workers in seven plants.)

One interesting vestibule program was created by Lockheed for operation in Sunnyvale, in the San Francisco Bay area. The aerospace company established a facility to train disadvantaged workers for jobs in 41 companies belonging to a consortium formed to provide financial support for the program. For a while at least, before Lockheed, along with other aerospace companies, ran into financial difficulties, many people hoped that the Sunnyvale program would prove to be a model corporate urban affairs project, and that the consortium formula would provide the key to success. Sadly, the corporate conscience was thwarted once again by the demands of the corporate balance sheets.

Community-Owned Subsidiaries

In order to assist economic development efforts in slum communities, several companies set up subsidiaries meant to be spun off for eventual ownership by neighborhood groups. These subsidiaries provide jobs and training for the disadvantaged right in the community. They are usually managed and supervised by blacks, and

[6] *The Wall Street Journal,* March 3, 1970.

[7] Lockheed's experience with programs for the disadvantaged is described in James D. Hodgson and Marshall H. Brenner, "Successful Experience: Training the Hard-Core Unemployed," *Harvard Business Review*, September-October 1968, pp. 148–56. Also see Jules Cohn, "The New Business of Business," *Urban Affairs Quarterly*, vol. 6, no. 1 (Fall 1970).

thereby also provide management training opportunities. Though only a handful of companies in the study chose this strategy for providing jobs and training, the community-owned subsidiary will be discussed here in some detail because of its potential significance in the drive to develop black and brown managers and entrepreneurs, and its popularity not only with community groups but with exponents of theories of black capitalism.

Setting up such a subsidiary requires an economic commitment greater than on-the-job or vestibule training programs. It also imposes a long-term moral responsibility on the parent company. The subsidiary has to be capitalized and supported until it can manage on its own. Therefore, the parent corporation must be a dependable purchaser or salesman of its products, through its own divisions, or its outside contacts. Some community-owned companies have received government contracts to get started, but most still depend on their parent companies, which must also, as a rule, provide advice on financial, production, marketing, and distribution practices.

Commitment to a subsidiary intended for community ownership involves the corporation in neighborhood relations on a greater scale than other kinds of training programs. Community groups become monitors of the enterprise and make demands and requests that corporate leaders sometimes view as intrusive or unnecessary. As a constituency these groups are quite different from average stockholders. For one thing, they aren't absent; they are right there, sometimes demanding a review of employment and operating procedures and other corporate policies. The subsidiary will one day be theirs, and they want to follow its progress, evaluating the implication of the parent's commitment. Companies that set up subsidiaries include:

- Aerojet-General, which established the Watts Manufacturing Company in Los Angeles in 1966. The project was originally funded by a $500,000 Labor Department job training grant, a $2.5 million Defense Department contract, and two government set-asides at $1.5 million. It began by employing about two hundred people.

- EG&G, which established a metal fabrication plant in the Roxbury section of Boston.
- Fairchild Hiller, which created FAIRMICCO, a metal, wood, and electrical fabricating plant in Washington, D.C. It had one hundred employees. Fairchild and Model Inner City Community Organization (MICCO), partners in the operation, were eventually to hold only 10 percent of the stock; most of the rest is for employees. FAIRMICCO was funded by Labor Department training grants and by the Economic Development Administration.
- Xerox, which, with other companies in Rochester, New York, established FIGHTON, a small manufacturing company. FIGHTON, owned by community stockholders, was given a large contract by Xerox.
- General Electric, which helped set up Progress Aerospace Enterprises, an electronic components manufacturing company in Philadelphia, managed by blacks, with a guarantee of business from GE.
- Mattel, which assisted Shindana Toys, a minority-owned business in Los Angeles. Shindana received management assistance from Mattel, as well as an initial credit line of $150,000.

Few of the subsidiaries intended for community ownership fared well. In the main, their problems were economic. EG&G's facility failed before it could be spun off to the community. There was considerable turmoil and strain, attributed to problems in management and financing. It closed in April 1970, at an estimated loss to the parent company of $500,000. Bernard J. O'Keefe, president of EG&G, blamed other businesses in the area, as well as the federal government, for failing to provide markets for the small company's products. "Everyone was hopped up over this thing 2 years ago," he said. "Company presidents would say, 'sure, we'll buy from you.' This would be passed down through vice presidents to the purchasing agent, whose job is to buy it at the lowest price. He'd give $500 to $1,000 worth of business, which is worse than nothing at all. I guess I know what blacks mean when they talk about tokenism."[8]

According to O'Keefe, EG&G underestimated the time and money needed to make a success of the project, and had difficulty, too, in finding the right managers. "This kind of venture attracts the people who are 'socially committed' and doing the job on their own time, but not the people who are concerned about costs or meeting budgets."[9]

Watts Manufacturing Company, created by Aerojet-General, also had problems but found someone to rescue it. The subsidiary was purchased from Aerojet in April 1970 by the Chase Manhattan Capital Corporation, a Small Business Investment Company (SBIC), for $1.1 million. Terms of the purchase provided that shares of the subsidiary would be placed in an escrow fund for eventual purchase by employees (most of whom are black) over a seven-year period. (Watts Manufacturing would thus continue to be eligible for contracts under the federal minority business procurement program.) The terms of the purchase provided that Chase would regain its equity as employees bought stock, but the SBIC would retain a 20 percent interest in the company. "It's a pretty fair business deal that should make money for everyone," said Louis L. Allen, CMCC president,[10] thus confirming that corporate conscience moves most readily when there are material incentives.

Company-Owned Subsidiaries

Wholly owned subsidiaries for training the disadvantaged were set up by North American Rockwell (NARTRANS in Los Angeles), Control Data (in North Minneapolis), AVCO Manufactur-

[8] *Business Week*, January 31, 1970.

[9] Quoted in *Fortune*, May 1970, p. 74.

[10] Quoted in *Business Week*, May 9, 1970, p. 26. For Allen's own report on earlier activities of Chase Manhattan's SBIC, see Louis L. Allen, "Making Capitalism Work in the Ghettos," *Harvard Business Review*, May-June 1969.

ing (in the Roxbury section of Boston), and about three dozen other companies. In many ways these subsidiaries are similar to those intended to be spun off: They are generally managed by non-whites, are designed on a small scale (fifty to two hundred employees), and obtain their production equipment from the parent company's surplus stock. But they are not meant for spinning off to the community, and are operated without participation by local groups.

Companies selecting this approach are attracted by the fact that by providing programs in separate facilities they can escape the need to alter ongoing production operations in existing locations. Whatever the special needs or problems of trainees, they do not interfere with the rest of the company. Only after careful screening, preceded by a period of training and actual work experience, are participants in these programs transferred into normal operations. It must be added that companies setting up such subsidiaries have been able to establish wage scales for the disadvantaged without consulting with union negotiators, who—at least to date—have been willing to exempt such separated operations from union agreements.

But both types of subsidiary introduce costs and complications avoidable in on-the-job training and vestibules. Once created, the new shop or factory has a life of its own, and an audience. It is harder to close down than a pilot training project using existing facilities in an existing plant. Its problems and achievements are more visible than those in programs that are part of normal operations. Constant care, including attention to its products and their marketing, as well as to the progress of training efforts, is needed in order to ward off the many problems that can arise.

Of the 247 companies in the study, only 11 set up subsidiaries. And the number of employees and trainees participating in them was small. A rough total of 1,000 disadvantaged workers are enrolled in the programs studied. Upgrading had been achieved for 125 employees, but few of these were transferred to jobs in parent companies.

TRAINING

Whatever the total number of jobs provided by industry's programs for the disadvantaged, there is ample evidence that the country's major companies can be induced to undertake some kind of minority recruiting and training effort. Key questions for businessmen but also for government policy makers are: What are the training requirements? How much will training cost? How can these costs be met?

Costs

When special training efforts are involved, employing the hard-to-employ entails higher costs than employing others. Companies sometimes pay for training of trainers and for orientation and training of supervisors. Auxiliary services—psychological counseling, remedial education, and social work—whether necessary or not, add to training costs, as well as expenditures for medical care and reimbursement for transportation, child care, etc. Accordingly, even companies with large training technologies incur new costs when they hire the disadvantaged.

Cost estimates vary widely, depending on the type of the company, its location, and the kind of training undertaken. Federal grants made under the JOBS program averaged $2,800 in 1968 and $3,000 in 1969 per trainee. But by the spring of 1970, this amount was cut back to $1,800. Companies supporting programs without government help report costs as high as $4,000 per trainee. Lowest costs are reported in the insurance and banking industries, where estimates are placed at $2,200 per trainee, compared to about $1,000 for other entry-level employees. Companies in the aerospace industry quote costs as high as $3,000 for each disadvantaged trainee, compared with $1,500 for other new hires. Costs of higher turnover and absenteeism contribute to company estimates.

Has any company not lost money on its programs? To date, no one has reported that hiring the disadvantaged has resulted in

56

direct economic benefits, but companies include in their calculations of the intangible return realized by their efforts such factors as enhancement of their reputation with consumers, government, and potential critics. And a few with urgent needs for unskilled labor have come to appreciate the value of the new manpower sources identified and developed by their programs.

For companies in the banking, insurance, and utilities industries, the improvement of training capabilities for the disadvantaged has led to improvements in training programs for other employees. And a limited number of companies are now producing goods and services formerly purchased on the open market, but now provided by the new employees during training periods. Though some companies have been accused of exploiting the JOBS program by claiming costs in excess of expenses incurred, other companies, including many large and prominent ones, have declined the opportunity to receive government benefits, and are paying for their programs themselves.

There are many reasons why a company might prefer to avoid participating in government-administered programs. A conscientious determination to pay its own bills rather than draw on public funds is, unfortunately, only one. Participants in the JOBS program must hire only those applicants cleared by government interviewers, and certified as meeting the criteria that define the disadvantaged. Many companies prefer to do their own screening, apply their own definitions, and avoid entanglement with public bureaucracy.

In his recent case study of IBM's new plant for disadvantaged workers in the Bedford-Stuyvesant section of Brooklyn, Edward C. Banfield called attention to the problem.[11] He reported a decision by the plant manager and his assistants to postpone the hiring of workers with serious problems until after a "productive" work force had been established. Friedli, the manager "was aware that the Management Review Committee expected him to dig deep into the hard core, as Eastman Kodak, for example, was doing. He

[11] Edward C. Banfield, "An Act of Corporate Citizenship," *Programs To Employ the Disadvantaged*, ed. Doeringer. pp. 26–57.

would dig eventually, but not right away."[12] The unmotivated, alcoholics, addicts, etc. would be avoided, at least in the beginning. Critics of the IBM effort offer another explanation, accusing the company of "creaming" the top of the labor supply in the neighborhood, to screen out the most disadvantaged.[13] Whatever the reason, the intrusion of government bureaucrats is considered by some companies to be more burdensome than paying the cost of hiring and training disadvantaged workers. Participation has also been inhibited by fears that payroll records, personnel folders, and training practices will be reviewed. Only a little more than half of the companies in the study with programs for the disadvantaged were operating them with the help of government funds.

Are the Auxiliary Services Needed?

In the business press and at workshops and seminars conducted by urban affairs consultants, poverty politicians, ideological academicians, and industrial and even clinical psychologists, the notion that the disadvantaged cannot be reached by normal techniques of manpower management has been popularized. A new technology of training is necessary, it is argued, and sizable investments are required to pay counselors, teachers, and sensitivity trainers. The government's own JOBS program legitimates (and stimulates) substantial training expenditures by providing subsidies for them, and for other services. Many companies known for their strong training capabilities (IBM, AT&T, and some of the aerospace companies) increased their already large training budget when they decided to recruit the disadvantaged.

But perhaps the training task is not as onerous or as costly as the literature and the sales talks of the consultants suggest. Jobs alone have motivated many members of the hard core, and vocational training alone without psychological support services has succeeded, too. The companies studied tried different techniques of training, at varying speeds. None reported that the key factor for success was

[12] *Ibid.*, p. 39.
[13] See John A. Hamilton, "The Business of Business Is Still Business," *New York Times,* February, 10, 1969, p. 38.

58

the provision of auxiliary services. "We learned that the real need was for revised techniques of training, not other services," said one company president.

It would appear from the data that it is not as difficult to motivate and train the disadvantaged as many people think. With retention rates at the 30-40 percent level, industry's programs prove that the performance of the hard core of the poor in entry-level jobs is not markedly inferior to that of other new employees. Many corporate leaders and line department heads, including personnel directors, feel that they were led to expect more severe training problems than they actually encountered.

THE FUTURE

The key challenge in corporate programs for the disadvantaged is how to pay for them, not how to conduct them. Costs need to be kept at levels reasonable enough to attract industry participation. Impassioned appeals for community service and alarming news reports from inner city neighborhoods will not be enough to sustain corporate interest in any program over the long term.

By stressing the importance of training and auxiliary services, rather than jobs alone, federal manpower policy has served to increase businessmen's expectations about the costs of programs and to influence the kinds of programs they create. The basic issue posed by the emphasis on training must, therefore, be resolved if realistic cost projections are to be made. Some suggest that the federal government ought to subsidize jobs rather than training. Senator Gaylord Nelson, chairman of the Subcommittee on Employment, Manpower, and Poverty of the Labor and Public Welfare Committee, has proposed that the Department of Labor earmark a portion of its budget allotment designated for manpower training to develop job programs instead, especially among the young. Other techniques that would shift government's emphasis onto jobs alone are needed.

It is possible that the basic problem faced by the disadvantaged is prejudice. If this is true, stronger government efforts to enforce antidiscrimination legislation are indicated, as well as efforts to reduce rather than exacerbate the anxieties of potential employers and co-workers about the special qualities of the disadvantaged. Stronger enforcement would encourage more companies to participate in hiring programs, particularly if extraneous training costs could be pared.

The business recession that began in the spring of 1970 proved that production cutbacks and slowdowns in industry are particularly hard on programs for the disadvantaged. Many companies terminated their programs, or refused appeals to begin new ones, blaming the recession for their negative attitudes. In addition to large layoffs at Chrysler, the recession has brought about dismissals at General Motors and in the steel industry.

Community group spokesmen and other urban crisis watchers interviewed have expressed concern that the recession and the layoffs it caused would lead to a resurgence of rioting and violence in the cities. The *New York Times* quoted Douglas Fraser, national director of the United Automobile Workers unit at Chrysler Corporation, as saying, "I just wonder whether we haven't done more harm than good with this program. We built up hopes and then we pull the rug out from under them."[14] But it is probably true that, if the recession continues and programs continue to be closed down, attempts to train and upgrade the disadvantaged will be defeated not by the problems of the trainees or the lack of skills on the part of their trainers, but by unrealistic cost schedules, ill-defined subsidy policies, and training definitions that make it impossible for programs to outlast a business slump.[15]

[14] *New York Times*, May 7, 1970.

[15] In early 1970 the NAB announced a new strategy to attract participation in the JOBS program by companies seen as immune to the recession. NAB would attempt to find jobs for the disadvantaged in service industries (schools, hospitals, and small businesses not directly dependent on manufacturing). Other companies enjoying "employment stability," such as the telephone companies, banks, and food processors, would be encouraged to participate. No reports on the outcome of this strategy have been issued.

5

Other Corporate Urban Programs

Twenty percent of the 247 companies in the nationwide study reported urban affairs activities in addition to, or instead of, donations or employment programs. These activities fall into three categories: (1) efforts to assist the economic development of central city slums, including loans or other assistance to schools, housing, and community corporations; (2) aid to individual minority group businessmen, mainly those who are black; and (3) programs that focus on other urban problems, including transportation, housing, environmental pollution, and the management needs of municipal governments. The main objective of programs in the latter group is to increase corporate income; the amelioration of city problems is a second aim, or a by-product of the first. These programs are conducted by companies eager to offer their products and services to meet demands created by city problems.

THE URBAN CRISIS AS A MARKET FOR CORPORATE SERVICES

In the vanguard of companies marketing their products as solutions to urban problems are those in the high technology industries, especially aerospace and electronics companies and manufacturers of computers and other scientific equipment. The urban crisis has also provided demands that can be filled by the building materials industry (including glass, gypsum, cement, lumber, and aluminum companies), as well as companies in the education industry and in management consulting. Twenty-nine companies said that their investment in programs to combat air and water pollution, to develop new technologies for the construction of low-cost housing, and to control and improve transportation, waste disposal, and educational systems constituted their contribution to urban affairs. In addition, nine companies reported projects in the application of systems analysis techniques to problems of local government. They described their work with cities on improving police capabilities, financial, health, hospital and school administration, and manpower management.

This section reports on the extent of these other urban affairs activities, discusses some of their implications for sponsoring companies, and comments on how if at all the private sector can provide solutions to public problems such as housing, education, and municipal administration.

Housing

All thirty-nine insurance companies in my study made pledges to the mortgage program created by their national association for the financing of low-cost housing construction. Other companies, including Alcoa, Johns-Manville, Westinghouse, Warner and Swasey, Reynolds Metal, United States Gypsum, U.S. Plywood-Champion Papers, American Standard, and Eastern Gas and Fuel Associates, have been contractors in urban renewal projects involving the construction of housing or commercial units in central city areas. Eli Goldston, president of Eastern Gas and Fuel, offers the following frank explanation of his company's participation in the Boston Urban Rehabilitation Program (BURP): "The decision to become involved . . . was made quite as much in response to financial and marketing opportunities as to moral exhortation to corporations for help in solving the urban crisis. As a part owner, we were able to specify gas for heating, cooking and water-heating in the rehabilitated units, thus creating for our subsidiary, Boston Gas Company, its largest single sales gain in recent years. . . . Our firm was able to consider the project as a major business task rather than as a secondary civic assignment or a hobby for a couple of executives."[1]

Through Operation Breakthrough, the federal government sought to induce industry to develop and undertake new approaches to low-cost housing construction. In December 1969, several dozen companies were designated "finalists" in the Department of Housing and Urban Development's contest for plans for inexpensive housing that could be built quickly and on a large scale. Westinghouse, General Electric, Alcoa, International Telegraph and Telephone, Boise-Cascade, Martin-Marietta, and U.S. Steel were among the companies submitting winning prototypes. But few of the computerized, systematized plans submitted by these companies, and doubtless technologically up-to-date, have resulted in housing units for the poor. The few projects that were completed, including that of Westinghouse's subsidiary, Urban Systems, Inc., are in suburban areas. Residents of slum neighborhoods have not yet received the benefits promised by elaborate plans still on the drawing boards of these giant companies.

Corporate managers interviewed in the spring of 1970 blamed the business recession for their inability to translate plans into action. "We cut our estimated costs down to the bone, and our profit projections, too," said a project manager in one of these companies. "But the guys in the head office want larger profits than our designs could ever produce. I'm afraid the poor will have to wait for the company's bottom line figures to increase. Or else the federal government will have to step in." An official of the Housing and Development Department passed the buck back to the executive suite: "The corporations want bigger carrots than we are able to offer them. The best we can do is get somebody to under-

[1] Eli Goldston, "New Prospects for American Business," *Daedalus*, Winter 1969, pp. 97–98.

take a pilot project by promising to mention his name in a press release."

Several companies have constructed new towns, advertised as total communities, with sections set aside for commercial and industrial, as well as residential and educational use. The premise of the new town movement seems to be that since the problems of existing cities are so overwhelming, the best solution is to build new cities.* Humble Oil, through a subsidiary, Friendswood Development, built Clear Lake City-Bayport, southeast of Houston, Texas. (Substantial initial incentive to Humble was provided by the government's plan to construct a spacecraft center in the same area.) On farmland halfway between Washington, D.C. and Baltimore, the Rouse Company created Columbia, Maryland. Other new town projects have been sponsored by Gulf, U.S. Steel, Alcoa, and Kaiser Industries and Kaiser Aluminum and Chemical Companies.

None of these new towns has helped the poor, except for the dubious benefit of removing some of the nonpoor from older cities. Those built to date are middle- and upper-middle class communities. Their residents have problems, but not those normally associated with the urban crisis. The boredom and blandness of life as part of a homogeneous population, and the limited range of choice in recreational and educational facilities are the crises with which they live.

By far the major investment in the planning and construction of housing for the poor, as well as schools, hospitals, and other institutional facilities for the central cities, has been made with public funds. Private enterprise has not yet found a profitable way to provide housing for low-income groups.

Rarely has an entrepreneur built housing deliberately for poor people. It is probably true, therefore, that decent homes for the urban poor will not become a reality in the absence of a major program of federally subsidized construction and rent. Thus the

* For an account of some of the complex issues raised by the new town idea, see Martha Derthick, "Defeat at Fort Lincoln," *The Public Interest*, no. 20 (Summer 1970), pp. 3–39.

problem of housing for the poor will have to be solved by the electorate and the politicians, not by corporate managers.[2]

Education

Many companies concentrate their urban affairs activities on the growing market for educational materials and services. They publish curriculum aids for urban schools, provide educational programs (or evaluate the programs of others), and conduct research. Westinghouse, General Electric, Avco, RCA, Litton Industries, Xerox, and Time, Inc. are among the large corporations selling educational services to local, state, or federal projects directly or through subsidiaries. Moreover, many smaller companies were created in the past few years by businessmen hoping to take advantage of the rising demand for textbooks and teaching materials. Among the other services they provide are the preparation and administration of training programs for disadvantaged employees, programed educational training for children and adults and in-service training of industry's employees. In addition, a management consulting firm in New York City was retained in the spring of 1970 by the Board of Education to help develop plans for decentralizing the city's school districts.

An increasing number of companies peddle programs offering the newest fashions in psychological services to personnel directors and line managers who believe that these tools will strengthen the performance of their employees, and thus improve company profits. Sensitivity training, psychodrama, exercises in role-playing can be bought, for example, from business school professors who describe themselves as "organization therapists," and are available on an hourly, per diem, or any other basis to corporate managers bitten by the psychology bug. They will massage the psyches of executives and employees in order to help a company improve its income. Dr. Frederick Herzberg of Western Reserve University, who writes a

[2] For a patrician, albeit sensible, discussion of some of the problems faced by real estate entrepreneurs who seek to make profits without doing harm to cities, see Roger Starr, *Urban Choices* (Baltimore: Penguin Books, 1966), pp. 86–92.

column in *Industry Week*, a publication available only to "top managers," has developed a theory of "motivation hygiene," which urges managers to provide employees with incentives in the work itself. Such a theory provides personnel directors with justifications for serving alleged psychological needs of workers, rather than material needs.[3] Though many of the motivation therapists minister mainly to bourgeois employees of large companies, they have countless counterparts who counsel the proletarian rather than the white collar ego.

Ecology

Environmental pollution is the most recent social issue to have attracted the attention of corporate managers. To some companies investment in environmental programs is more attractive than expenditures for programs to train disadvantaged workers or to assist community economic development efforts. Ecology is a safe issue for companies where racial, ethnic, or religious bias is still strong, or where at the top-level there is resistance to involvement in urban economic issues.* Investment in ecological programs by

[3] See Frederick Herzberg, *Work and the Nature of Man* (Cleveland: The World Publishing Company, 1966), for an exposition of his doctrine.

* In the conspiracy-theory tradition, Norman Podhoretz offers another explanation for the popularity of ecology as an urban affairs issue. "The environment . . . is the issue on which the WASP patriciate . . . hopes to reassert its primacy in general and, in particular, to recapture the Republican Party and the White House from the forces that now hold them both in such precarious captivity." Podhoretz took the proclamation of Earth Day as a starting-off point for an essay about the motives of supporters of the rite, including John Gardner and John V. Lindsay. "The truth is that the environment . . . has since the days of Theodore Roosevelt . . . been a cause dear to the hearts of the WASP patricians. It is an issue which focuses in a very precise and uniquely poignant way their perennial protest against what they have always seen as the despoliation of the national estate by the selfish interests that were enthroned in the Gilded Age. That these interests were enthroned at the political expense of the WASP patriciate has never seemed to it a reason for suspecting that an element of the self-servingly tendentious might have entered into its assessment of the situation . . . Its only interest, it devoutly believes, is the Public Interest, and it sees itself as the only group in the country which has only the public interest at heart." Norman Podhoretz, "Reflections on Earth Day," *Commentary,* vol. 49, no. 6 (June 1970) pp. 26–28.

some companies is probably a cop-out, an attempt to win credit for corporate citizenship without tackling issues that would seem to deserve higher priority.

Pressure is increasing on companies in pollution-producing industries to diminish their abuse of the environment or to call a halt completely to operations that pollute. Measures to eliminate lead from their petroleum products or to remove industrial waste without polluting rivers and waterways are reported as urban affairs efforts by many companies in an attempt to win credit merely for trying to meet legal requirements.

Management Advice to Local Governments

A small number (seven) of the companies included in the study said that providing management consulting services to city governments is their main urban affairs effort. Two of these companies are in the aerospace industry; the others are in electronics, appliances, or computer manufacturing. In addition to the companies interviewed, many accounting, engineering, and management consulting firms are engaged in projects commissioned by mayors, budget directors, police, hospitals, health, fire, sanitation, transportation, housing, welfare, and personnel departments in cities throughout the country.

In some cities, consultant contracts to private firms constitute a sizable portion of the municipal budget. In New York, for example, in 1969, architectural and engineering contracts amounting to nearly $32 million were awarded by the Budget Bureau.[4] Other consultant services, including the advice of accounting, management, and systems analysis and development organizations, were retained for a total of nearly $33 million.[5] Under the administration of Mayor John V. Lindsay, the city is said to have increased its

[4] Quoted from data provided by the Office of the Comptroller, City of New York, June 1970.

[5] *New York Times*, August 10, 1970.

expenditures for outside consultants from $8 million in 1965 to $7 million in 1969.[6]

Consulting firms provide a wide variety of services to city governments. In Los Angeles, New York, Cleveland, Boston, and Cincinnati, management firms have designed information systems for mayors, command and control techniques for police departments, governmental reorganization plans, and new city-wide salary schedules. For sanitation departments, they have provided manpower deployment plans, and for budget and tax bureaus, advice on fiscal management. (In New York, one firm was retained by city officials administering the Model Cities program, though the use of management consultants would seem inconsistent with the spirit of the program. Model Cities, after all, was set up to encourage participation in planning by community groups rather than by professional advisors.)

Management consultants and systems analysts are attracted to the urban crisis by the powerful incentives provided by: (1) their civic consciences; (2) their eagerness to respond to a new challenge to their experience and skills; and (3) a new opportunity to fatten their purses. The reasons for their appeal to city officials call for other explanations. Mayors, commissioners, and other political executives quite naturally seek help when frustrated by the rate at which their problems increase. In an earlier era, they would have had to rely on the advice and services of political appointees, but now they have another option, for an advice industry has burgeoned in the public sector, eager for mayoral patronage, and ready to offer pleasure to political patrons. The business consultants, who heretofore limited their activities to industrial organizations, are now found in the corridors of city halls. And mayors have seen some advantages in welcoming these new consultants, whose wares are said to be the products of detached, technically proficient, and fearless problem-solving. The consultant claims that his view of a city's problems is objective, transcending partisanship or organizational

[6] *Ibid.*

identification. Central to his creed (and his career) is the theme that all problems can be solved—not just identified or controlled. With his sometimes dazzling devices of systems analysis, decision trees, computer programs, and his special understanding of organizational life, he brings hope, reassurance, and even emotional support to harried albeit naïve clients. And today's big-city mayor is surely as harried as a top corporate ruler.

Important questions arise about the work of management consultants in city government and urban affairs. For whom do these technical advisers speak? Are the solutions they propose adequate to the problem or merely designed to comfort, or win reelection for, the client? For what is good for a mayor may not necessarily be useful to his constituents. An approach to cost-cutting that is appropriate in General Motors could be harmful in a public agency where some considerations must outweigh slide-rule calculations. A city's obligations as an employer are different from those of an industrial corporation; efficiency in a city's hospitals cannot be defined the same way as efficiency for a product manager in a drug company. It is incumbent on the consultant, because he commutes between commercial and governmental clients, to face the responsibility of distinguishing between the needs and values of the two environments. (The burden on mayors is heavy, too; they must stand ready to challenge or reject the consultants' recommendations.)

Executives in engineering, aerospace, computer, and management consulting firms were optimistic about their ability to help the cities solve their problems. They insist that their work is nonpolitical and nonpartisan, but this is likely to be attacked as the number of contracts they receive increases. For while there can be no argument about the cities' need for help in managing programs, the assumption that a private firm's "systems" or "analytical" advice to a political executive can be objective, showing no partisan bias, will not be shared by officers of firms left out in the cold, or by good-government watchdogs of mayoral budgets and city hall patronage.

COMMUNITY ECONOMIC DEVELOPMENT

Twelve percent of the companies I studied are involved in efforts designed to improve economic conditions in slum communities, nowadays erroneously referred to as ghettoes. Some of these efforts take the form of loans or management assistance for the improvement of housing, schools, transportation, and health services. A few companies have located a plant or other facility in a slum neighborhood in order to provide jobs and economic upgrading opportunities. Companies have set up neighborhood information centers to refer community residents to a wide range of services— housing, medical treatment, job placement, etc. Citizens and Southern National Bank in Savannah, Georgia, for example, formed a local development corporation to provide loans for down payments on mortgages by low-income people, and to extend equity capital to small businessmen. Demonstration day-care centers and playgrounds, as well as housing rehabilitation projects, are other activities of its development corporation.

Prospects for a government-subsidized day-care program in which profit-making firms can participate have stimulated some companies to develop plans and apply their skills to another urban need. In Massachusetts, both KLH and Avco operated child-care centers, established to provide incentives for mothers to take jobs in their plants. A spokesman for KLH's Child Development Center explained the company's motivation: The "labor pool is expanded and absenteeism declines. Day care cuts down on family-related anxieties when a mother can see her child at lunchtime, and that results in greater productivity."[7] (Only a few dozen children are enrolled in KLH's program, which is not designed to provide income.)

Central city high schools have been "adopted" by a handful of insurance companies, utilities, and banks. In Hartford, Aetna Life and Casualty Insurance provides free space and facilities to Weaver

[7] Quoted in *Business Week*, March 21, 1970, p. 112.

High, as well as some vocational courses. Michigan Bell Telephone reported that it offers training courses to students in Northern High, a predominantly black school in a slum community in Detroit. Chicago's Commonwealth Edison set up a program for its employees to serve as tutors of students in schools in slum neighborhoods. Among the companies that established plants in poverty areas or seek to improve local economic conditions in other ways are Control Data (Minneapolis), Avoc (Roxbury, Boston), General Dynamics (San Antonio), J. C. Penney (St. Louis), and Westinghouse Electric (Pittsburgh). Almost all these corporate programs in slum areas were begun in 1968 and early 1969, when the memory of urban disorders was fresh in the minds of businessmen.

Proposals for government subsidies for firms willing to locate in poverty areas have been discussed frequently since 1967. It is probably safe to assume that unless such incentives are provided, businessmen will not be motivated to undertake major investments in depressed neighborhoods. Decisions about site selection are basically economic, calling for consideration of land costs, tax policies, market availability, and labor supply. The need to respond to fears and anxieties provoked by riots will be considered as the primary criterion only when there appear to be major threats to corporate security.[8] Locational decisions favoring slum neighborhoods can be encouraged by wage and training subsidies, and government programs to improve transportation facilities that connect slum neighborhoods with areas where jobs are available. But as one commentator has observed, "to the extent that industrial location drives real estate prices up, adds to traffic congestion, uproots people from their homes and brings industry into residential areas [it] may have distinctly harmful effects on the neighborhood which may not be offset by the advantage of . . . additional employment opportunities."[9]

[8] See William K. Tabb, "Government Incentives to Private Industry to Locate in Urban Poverty Areas," *Land Economics*, November 1969, pp. 392–99.

[9] *Ibid.*, p. 399.

PROMOTING BLACK CAPITALISM

One of the most controversial strategies proposed for solution of urban problems is based on the ideology of black capitalism, the belief that to cure the ills of the cities, the number and power of black or brown capitalists must be increased. Black capitalism is warmly endorsed by such corporate leaders as James M. Roche, chairman of the board of General Motors. "It is for us," he said, "who have worked within and gained from the free enterprise system, to help others to share in it. It is for us, who most cherish the freedom in free enterprise, to assure that it is freely open to everyone."[10] A handful of corporations have been sufficiently persuaded by this ideology to sponsor the formation of businesses owned and operated by blacks. Assistance in the form of guaranteed purchase orders, loans, or management advice is offered to aspiring black entrepreneurs. Xerox Corporation, Fairchild Hiller, Eastern Gas and Fuel, Mattel Toys, and General Electric are among the companies that have embarked on such efforts.

Other companies have made "technical assistance" available to businesses owned by blacks. Swift and Company told of helping blacks establish ice-cream parlors in Chicago; Safeway Stores, Inc. reported that it purchases produce from a black-owned cooperative in Louisiana. Banks told of their efforts to identify and assist black businessmen with credit and advice. Several major petroleum companies cited promises made in the fall of 1969 to increase the number of service station franchises held by blacks. According to the Commerce Department, minorities (meaning blacks, mainly) owned only 5.5 percent of the country's 250,000 service stations. The industry agreed to increase that number by 1974 to 10 percent. (But as of June 1970, the government observed that the twenty major oil companies who signed up for the program had "begun slowly."[11])

The Commerce Department initiated a program whereby it would provide matching funds and guaranteed bank loans to companies

[10] *Business and Society*, vol. 2, no. 15 (January 27, 1970), p. 2.
[11] *New York Times*, June 29, 1970.

setting up a MESBIC (Minority Enterprise Small Businessmen Investment Corporation), a subsidiary that in turn would extend credit to minority-owned business. The program has led to the creation of a handful of MESBICs that have extended credit to three or four dozen minority-owned companies. General Motors, Prudential Insurance, Arcata Investment, and Varian have carried out pledges to set up investment companies. But many of the major corporations that said they would participate in the program have not yet done so. The results, therefore, are far from spectacular. Though the Commerce Department predicted in the fall of 1969 that one-hundred companies would be in the program by June 30, 1970, providing financial leverage up to $500 million, only nine companies kept their pledges by that date, with commitments at only $150,000 each. Nor had all nine granted loans.[12] "I think we've made extraordinary progress, considering the state of the economy," said Under Secretary of Commerce Rocco C. Siciliano. "It's hard to imbue businessmen with social consciousness when business is bad."[13]

Among proponents of minority business development is Darwin W. Bolden, national executive director of the Interracial Council for Business Opportunity (ICBO). According to Bolden, the "basic responsibility for fostering minority entrepreneurship rests with the private sector."[14] ICBO, founded by the Urban League and the American Jewish Congress, recruits volunteer consultants from the corporate world to provide advice to black and brown businessmen. It recently formed a referral service for big companies interested in doing business with black entrepreneurs. In addition, ICBO provides assistance in developing new markets and packaging business properties for financing, and provides direct financing through its own capital tools. In its seven years of existence, it has generated approximately $15 million in debt and equity financing of more than four hundred new businesses and thirty-five existing businesses.

[12] *Ibid.*
[13] *Ibid.*
[14] Quoted in *Business and Society* vol. 2, no. 15 (January 27, 1970).

Theodore Cross's proposals for the encouragement of black capitalism argue for the development of devices to enable black businessmen to obtain large amounts of credit, commitments of risk capital, and training in marketing and production skills.[15] Cross has recommended tax credits for lenders willing to assume the risks presented by inexperienced minority group businessmen and other incentives to stimulate deposits in ghetto banks and to spur the financing of black-owned businesses.

The ideology of black capitalism implies separatist rather than integrationist means to solving urban problems. Needless to say, there is a tremendous need for assistance to black businessmen, in all the forms suggested by proponents of this ideology. But other urban problems are equally compelling, especially those faced by the poor. Black capitalism will help aspiring entreprenuers but will not provide low-cost housing, or pay for improvement in urban education, and other social programs. Big business and government can support these programs now, while at the same time aiding the development of black entrepreneurs. Yet some ideologues oppose such programs, deriding them as "integrationist" solutions. Oddly enough, black capitalism has attracted the interest of some members of the business community more than other urban projects. Perhaps this is because it seems to be no threat to the corporate world, since its supporters do not demand jobs, nor do they discuss more radical solutions—such as, reparations payments or restructuring of large companies to provide a degree of community control. In short, black capitalism has "peculiar merit," in Sumner Rosen's phrase, for corporate leaders.[16]

It is not clear how emphasis on slum economic development programs or on black capitalism will help remove or even reduce racial barriers in housing and employment, or for that matter how such emphasis will provide more jobs, better schools, health and hospital care, or protection for the low-income consumer.

[15] See Theodore L. Cross, *Black Capitalism* (New York: Atheneum, 1969).

[16] Sumner M. Rosen, "Better Mousetraps," *Urban Review*, May 1970, pp. 15–18.

6

Urban Affairs Organization Men

Indications of the importance of a corporate function are provided by the position it occupies on the organization chart and the types of people charged with implementing it. This chapter discusses the organizational status and roles of urban affairs officers, as well as their educational backgrounds, work experience, and career goals. In addition, it comments on some of the problems faced by the idealistic urban affairs officer seeking to serve his company without violating his conscience.

URBAN AFFAIRS IN THE CORPORATE ORGANIZATION

In all but 46 of the 247 companies studied, full- or part-time responsibility for urban affairs was formally assigned to someone; only two of these assignments were made before 1967, when the Kerner Commission was appointed. The assignment is most frequently found in the personnel department (67 companies). Next most popular locations were public relations (40) and public or government affairs (38). (See diagram below.)

Assigning urban affairs to personnel is a logical choice for companies whose urban affairs programs are limited to increased hir-

Exhibit IV

Responsibility for urban affairs:
where it is assigned in 247 companies

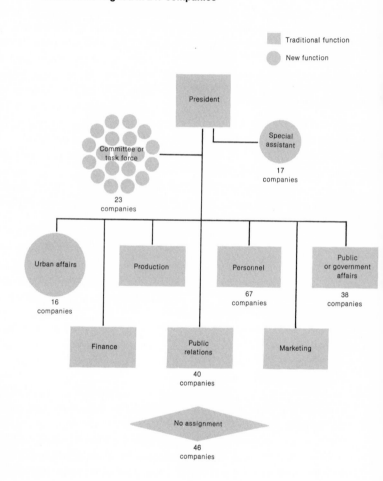

Traditional function

New function

President

Special
assistant

17
companies

Committee or
task force

23
companies

Urban affairs

16
companies

Production

Personnel

67
companies

Public
or government
affairs

38
companies

Finance

Public
relations

40
companies

Marketing

No assignment

46
companies

ing of minority group members. In these companies, the chief responsibility of the urban affairs executive (sometimes called minority group adviser or employee relations director) is to develop recruitment programs. As indicated in Chapter 3, the phrase "minority group members" tends to mean those who are black or speak Spanish. None of the urban affairs officers interviewed said that his responsibilities included services to white minority group members, the ethnic Americans. "The Irish and Italians will have to fend for themselves," said the minority group adviser in a large insurance company in New Jersey. "They have a few years' head start, and at least know the ground rules of the rat race."

In some companies, a troubleshooter role was created to ward off criticism of recruitment and advancement practices affecting blacks. An executive would be assigned to look out for their interests, and to act as a broker through whom aggrieved employees could communicate to top management.[1]

In several companies an adviser on minority affairs was appointed to act as a gadfly inside the organization, monitoring progress and trying to stimulate program activity. Many interviewees said they were expected to play this role, and be in-house advocates of urban affairs efforts. Few found the role an easy one. In the absence of line authority or a formal means of exercising power and influence on employment policies, they must rely on informal techniques, and need constant support from line officers and the chief executive. Clearly such a role has built-in limitations, and leads to personal conflicts similar to those faced by priests at courts, or by company psychologists, all of whom have to serve patrons as well as clients. They owe allegiance to their vocation, but are on the payroll of a corporate organization.

Those companies assigning the urban affairs function to public relations departments flatly admit that their main interest is in improving their reputations rather than personnel practices. "My job

[1] Soon after fourteen nonwhite employees filed charges of discrimination against the Chase Manhattan Bank in New York, a department of staff development was created to improve grievance procedures and assist the advancement of nonwhite employees to management positions.

is to anticipate and prevent conflict between the company and the community," said an urban affairs man in a public relations slot, "and to beat the drum about what a great company we are."

In 40 companies out of the 247, urban affairs work consisted chiefly of preparing brochures and writing speeches. Nearly all big companies now provide the public with pamphlets, booklets, and other puffy pronouncements of their urban affairs activities.

Companies worried about protecting their good names with government agencies place the urban affairs role under the aegis of the lobbyist—the government relations staff or the legislative liaison office. Companies in industries that rely heavily on government contracts—aerospace, scientific equipment, and computer manufacturers—assign urban affairs responsibilities to the executives who manage relations with public agencies. Similarly, those closely regulated by government or beneficiaries of publicly protected advantages—such as, food and drug, chemicals, and petroleum industries—also deposit urban affairs personnel in departments that deal with bureaucrats and legislators.

In twenty-three of the companies studied, urban affairs responsibilities were delegated to a "task force" of officers from several departments. "We didn't know where to put it, so we formed a committee," said a New York banker. Most of these companies said their committees were a temporary measure, to be replaced eventually by a departmental assignment. A spokesman for a nationwide supermarket chain offered the following reason for forming a committee: "We had run up a $200,000 urban affairs bill," he said. "We were conducting 14 training programs on the East Coast for nonwhite cashiers and clerks, negotiating with three community groups who were boycotting us for selling California grapes, and preparing an advertising campaign to persuade black customers in low income neighborhoods that we were not the enemy. Each of these activities had to be monitored by different people in corporate headquarters, and we thought a coordinating structure was needed. So we set up a committee."

In sixteen companies, some of whom had already tried the committee approach, a new department for urban affairs was created.

"We didn't want our urban affairs man locked into personnel or PR work exclusively," said one senior executive. "Urban affairs ought to have a niche of its own." Another reported, "Urban affairs officers can be buried as quickly as they are born. In this company, we could have accomplished that by assigning the man to personnel. No one gets out of there alive."

THE CORPORATE URBAN AFFAIRS OFFICER

Most of the new urban affairs departments are run by former personnel or public relations officials. Seventeen companies designated special assistants for urban affairs who report to the chief executive. The duties of these assistants include speechwriting, reviewing requests for donations, meeting with community groups, and interpreting the company's interest in urban affairs to line executives. "I thought I'd like to have a right-hand man especially assigned to it," said one company president. "My assistant keeps me abreast of urban issues and our problems and progress. I'll probably bureaucratize him eventually, by converting him and the assignment into a department."

The reporting relationship indicates the relative importance of any job in a large company. Urban affairs is no exception. When it reports at the presidential or vice-presidential levels, its status and power is highest. In addition to the seventeen companies in the study with urban affairs assistants to the president, five heads of urban affairs departments also report to the president. A little less than half of all the other urban affairs men report at the vice-presidential level.

To learn more about the men (there were no women) charged with urban affairs responsibilities, eighty-three of these executives were interviewed, and many more were asked to complete questionnaires. Data were sought about their training, social and political values, and career goals. Are they organization men with little interest in urban problems, or social reformers who infiltrated the corporate world?

The typical urban affairs man is in his early thirties. He has had a few other jobs before moving into his current one, but none was related to urban affairs. He eventually plans to move on to another, more important role in the company. His career is in the company, not in urban affairs. The chances are ten to one that he is white.

Several executives indicated that they viewed urban affairs as a job for young managers, rather than older, seasoned, or highly experienced ones. "Young people have a better feeling for urban problems than do middle-aged officers," said the chief executive of a San Francisco company known for active work in urban affairs. "I see an urban affairs post as a starting-point for our men, where they can learn about the company." While no fiery-eyed evangelists were found among corporate urban affairs officers, roughly half of those interviewed insisted on their enthusiasm, even excitement, for the assignment. A few saw it as an opportunity to amend corporate life, making it pleasanter for employees. "The message I want to transmit to the top is that what's good for disadvantaged trainees is good for all employees," said one young urban affairs officer, "but I don't know if the C.E.O. [chief executive officer] hears us." Many people privately expressed skepticism about industry's willingness and ability to stick with the programs already begun. Speculations that urban affairs is only a passing phase rather than a long-term commitment in some companies was frequently heard.

Most of the younger people saw their jobs as a career opportunity—a place to get exposure and to make contacts, both within the company and outside. Older men, on the other hand, saw them as a good berth, especially after work in high-pressure jobs. Only seven of all those interviewed said they planned to spend their careers in urban affairs. "If the action were in some other sphere, I'd be there," said a thirty-year-old vice-president of personnel. "I'll hand the urban job over to someone else as soon as this company's interest begins to wane." Many of the youngest officers expressed a view combining opportunism and idealism. A stint in urban affairs is rather like a tour of duty in the Peace Corps: two years off in a strange land as a do-gooder, followed by a return to the pursuit of career ambitions.

Energetic Amateurs

Most urban affairs officers are amateurs in their work; only five had any experience or relevant training before assuming their roles. All are college graduates with majors mainly in business subjects. A few had studied sociology, political science, or history. A handful of companies sought specialists, or nonbusiness types, for their urban affairs departments. One urban affairs man is a Peace Corps alumnus; an airline recruited a former congressional aide; and a retail chain hired a city planner. Still other companies hired city managers, college professors, and lawyers for urban affairs jobs. "The possibility of urban affairs work helps us attract young people who otherwise might not be interested in us," said one company spokesman. In general, the business schools provide candidates for urban affairs, along with other corporate jobs. Whether or not they offer appropriate training for these posts is questionable. These schools train their students for managerial or entrepreneurial roles, not for analysis or understanding of urban problems. Significantly, most of the advances made in social policy in the field of manpower development have been made possible by research and recommendations presented by social scientists, few of whom have ever been near a business school. At most, the young M.B.A.s holding urban affairs posts to whom I talked were energetic and public spirited amateurs, unprepared by exposure or training for the problems they seek to solve.

The Fate of the Urban Affairs Man

Appointment to an urban affairs position, according to some of the men interviewed, is not always an advancement or career opportunity. Some former line executives now head urban affairs departments: a one-time vice-president for marketing, for whom the job was a demotion, and a soon-to-retire senior vice-president, who described it as the pasture in which he had been put to rest. "I'm not sure whether I was promoted or shoved aside," said the new urban affairs officer in a large petroleum company. He had been transferred from a marketing position in the field to head a new urban affairs headquarters staff. Nor was it clear that he knew very much about urban affairs, even though no one doubted that he knew a lot about oil.

Because of the ambiguity of the role and its newness in most companies, some incumbents worry about their jobs being dead-end: "If I didn't really care about urban issues, it would be easy to spend too much time wondering if this job is the end of my climb in this company."

In some corporations, of course, genuine interest by top management can make the urban affairs role an important and coveted one. But in only five of the companies studied was the new urban affairs department given a commitment of resources, funds, and talent thought impressive by company insiders. In these companies, the job would be attractive to anyone on the way up. Executives in these jobs may not be able to do much good for the cities, but as a result of top management interest in community problems, some of them find their careers enhanced by the exposure granted to them by the urban crisis.

7

Clark Corporation and the Disadvantaged: A Case Study

INTRODUCTION

This is an account of a corporate adventure in social development. It is the story of the effort by a leading corporation to create and sustain a program to hire and train the disadvantaged. The subsidiary described here was one of about thirty other efforts undertaken by American industry in the period 1967–70. Soon after they were established, many of these programs encountered difficulties. Several have already been terminated. Of those that survive, few can be described as successful. Leaders of sponsoring corporations, once optimistic about what they could do, now emphasize the many problems involved. Some of these problems and the reasons for them are described here.*

PHONE CALL FROM THE WHITE HOUSE

In October 1967, John Button, president of Planet Corporation, a major aerospace company on the West Coast, received a telephone call from the White House. The Johnson Administration, he was told, wanted Planet to join the list of large companies

---

* The case is based on actual events, and only the names of the individuals and companies involved have been changed.

pledged to cooperate in a nationwide effort to offer jobs and training to the disadvantaged. Planet was a likely choice for the government caller. It is one of the country's largest industrial corporations, ranking in the top fifty of *Fortune*'s list of five hundred largest industrials. It has divisions in several large American cities where there had been summer riots. Moreover, in recent years, it has received defense contracts amounting to millions of dollars.

Button readily agreed to cooperate with the government's request. He had described himself in a newspaper interview a few years earlier as a "statesman of capitalism." He was a board member of the local Urban Coalition and a member of the task force of the regional organization of the National Alliance of Businessmen. "I spent my first thirty years worshiping the golden calf," he told me. "I worked hard enough to pay for all the comforts I'll need for the rest of my life. I jump at every chance to do something for the community."

Button was sure that Planet could successfully train the hard core. The company's training resources were a source of pride. "We've always been proud of our ability to train. During the war, we taught women to be first-rate riveters. When the labor supply in the cities tightened up, we brought farmhands in from the Southwest. Though they had never even seen a factory, we prepared them for assembly-line jobs."

Button was confident that the private sector could effectively cope with the problems which had been frustrating public authorities. His view was shared by many other company presidents and board chairmen in the aftermath of the riots. For businessmen all over the country were pledging to conduct special training programs. In Detroit, for example, Ford and General Motors announced that they would hire and train thousands of hard-core workers. In New York, IBM announced the opening of a new plant in the Bedford-Stuyvesant section of Brooklyn that would provide jobs and training for the poor.

After saying "yes" to the White House, Button directed his staff to prepare a program recommendation. Six weeks later, a memorandum was on his desk from Earl Dunsany, senior vice-president for administration, recommending that Planet set up a training subsidiary to produce goods and services for its parent divisions. Other approaches to training, including on-the-job and vestibule programs, were rejected in the memorandum. Dunsany believed that the latter alternatives would not provide adequate time or resources. A subsidiary, he argued, was desirable because it would offer a realistic training environment. The memorandum rejected on-the-job training on the grounds that it required workers to compete with production pressures for the attention of their trainers. The vestibule was rejected because it is an artificial environment, cut off from actual production processes. "We wanted a real factory, not a simulated one," said Dunsany.

To be sure, the subsidiary approach was attractive for other reasons, too. Disadvantaged employees would be isolated from other production workers at Planet, protecting the parent company from the hostility of the latter that might arise if they felt they were denied privileges granted to the former. Furthermore, by creating a separate unit whose employees were recruited through government agencies, Planet hoped to secure cooperation from union officials. If trainees were brought into normal operations, the company could be accused of undercutting standard wage scales, for the new workers would be paid at rates lower than those prevailing in other divisions.

PLANNING, FINANCING, AND STAFFING THE SUBSIDIARY

In March 1968, Planet announced the incorporation of its wholly owned subsidiary to "help disadvantaged people help themselves." The new company would be called Clark Corporation, to honor the first president of Planet, Button's maternal grandfather, Higbert "Golden Rule" Clark, a real estate developer who had also founded the oldest local charity. The subsidiary's objective was to provide two hundred jobs in a facility located in or near a poverty area. Clark would:

- Provide products and services needed by Planet's divisions.
- Provide "industrially and commercially salable" work experience for disadvantaged employees and develop "solid attitudes toward employment." As workers gained skill and experience, they would be transferred to Planet's divisions and be replaced by new trainees.

To staff the project, Button tapped managerial talent within the parent company. Dunsany, the project's chief planner and developer, became president and board chairman of Clark. Foster Williams, an engineer with fifteen years of experience as a group manager in one of Planet's divisions, was named vice-president and general manager. Williams would run the plant, reporting directly to Dunsany at Planet. Though Williams is black, Planet insisted that he was chosen because of his experience in production supervision, not his color.

"I was interested in the hard core," he later said. "but had little knowledge of their problems." Williams was born in a southern city, to parents whom he described as "working people." "We were hard-working and sometimes hard-up, but never hard core." After graduation from college, where he was supported by the G.I. bill, he left the South to find work as an engineer.

After a series of meetings with Button and Dunsany, followed by a round of press conferences to announce the formation of Clark Corporation, Williams selected his staff. He hired a white engineer, who had worked for him at Planet, as his special assistant. Ten out of sixteen supervisors also came from Planet. None had worked with hard-core employees, but as Williams knew, few supervisors in industry had. Only two were nonwhite. A staff was hired to perform personnel, accounting, and clerical functions. Two white teachers experienced in work with nonwhite students were also hired.

Clark was to be located in an old warehouse, for which Dunsany had signed a five-year lease, in an industrial district near the center of town. The building was five stories high, and occupied about one-third of a city block halfway between an old railroad siding and a large frozen foods processing plant. Floor space was 84,000 square feet. By the standards of white-collar workers, or any other middle-class observers, the building and its surroundings were drab. But the rent was low, and the location would be convenient for employees, who would be able to travel to work on a short bus trip from the central city. If there would be complaints about the location, they would come from managers and supervisors, who would have to forego the conveniences and comforts in facilities of Planet headquarters in a much better part of town. Because there were no restaurants nearby, Clark's employees would have to depend on the coffee and sandwich vendors who visit the area during mealtimes. Executives in search of expense-account lunches would have to drive to the other side of the tracks.

Dunsany arranged to have Planet's divisions supply most of the machinery and hardware that would be needed to begin production. Planet committed nearly $500,000 in equity to Clark. About $200,000 of this amount went for improvements on the building itself. Another $75,000 was spent on machinery and equipment, most of which was contributed by other Planet divisions at book value.

Ongoing financial support to cover the difference between normal training costs and the cost of training the disadvantaged was secured by a contract under the Manpower Development and Training Act (MDTA) with the Department of Labor. The contract provided for federal subsidies at the rate of $2,900 per trainee to cover the costs of vocational training, remedial reading and writing courses, physical examinations (including eyeglasses when necessary), and transportation during the first weeks of training. The contract required that Planet hire only employees certified by the Concentrated Employment Program (CEP) operated in conjunction with the State Employment Service.

The long-range objective of Clark was to operate at break-even levels. Goods and services were to be provided to Planet divisions at full cost and in sufficient volume to cover all overhead, excluding training expenses reimbursable under the MDTA contract. To the extent that the divisions did not generate sufficient orders for

Clark products, the subsidiary's underabsorbed overhead (including unbilled direct labor time) was to be charged back to them. Thus Clark and the divisions of the parent company were tied together in a cleverly contrived economic symbiosis. The divisions would be charged outright for Clark's operations, unless they found ways of providing it with enough work. Even then, if Clark had to charge them above-the-market rates, they would be penalized. These arrangements were soon to create tensions between the new company and divisions of the older one. As some division spokesmen saw it, they were forced, by order of Planet's president, to be guardians of "his stepchild," as they sometimes referred to Clark. And Williams and his staff, when they complained about the divisions, characterized them as "our big stepbrothers in corporate headquarters." It certainly was true that Button created Clark to demonstrate his own convictions about the need for positive expressions of corporate citizenship in a time of urban crisis. But the financial plan by which Clark would be maintained made clear to his division chiefs that they would have to pay for convictions that he had expressed merely in words.

To guarantee continued concern by division heads, and to enforce the commitment of an adequate volume of work orders, the senior vice-presidents of the divisions were named directors of Clark. In addition, division heads were asked to provide managerial and financial advice to Williams.

The initial operating plan for fiscal year 1969 called for:

- Sales (work orders) from Planet divisions to support 240,000 direct labor hours, based upon a planned labor efficiency of 60 percent (60 percent of normal worker productivity).
- Total salary and wage payments, and related benefits, of approximately $2 million, of which:
  - $560,000 would be absorbed in product costs as direct labor;
  - $360,000 would be reimbursed under the MDTA contract; and

———— Approximately $1 million would be expended on management and supervisory staff salaries and training expenses. This amount would be recovered by an applied overhead rate of $6.00 per direct labor hour (about 250 percent of labor wage rates).

The minimum hourly wage was set at $2.10; the maximum was set at $2.50. These wages were high enough to attract people on welfare and also to compete with area pay scales. They were low enough to account for the fact that productivity would probably be 60 to 70 percent of normal.

The cost schedule was intended to allow Clark's prices to be reasonably competitive. After allowing for the 60 percent utilization, costs approximated those incurred by other firms, and while overhead rates were high, the absence of a required profit margin tended to compensate.

In summary, an accounting system was devised that provided for the support of Clark at no cost to Planet. If the divisions fulfilled their obligation to purchase goods and services at required rates, and if the federal government paid the costs of screening, training, and counseling, Clark would at least be a bookkeeping success. Whether it would succeed in its mission to assist the disadvantaged was another question.

Moving In

Williams and his new staff and supervisors moved into the plant as soon as repairs were completed. They held a series of meetings with officials of the State Employment Service to learn how job candidates were screened under provisions of the MDTA contract and to agree on procedures by which candidates would be referred to them. Each of the two local offices of CEP had a backlog of certified applicants ready for referral, and the agency's staff was eager to "move them through the pipeline," as one official put it. As soon as Williams was ready to start operations, he was to notify these offices. Clark would have the right to reject two out of three applicants, but could not hire anyone who lacked CEP certification. Even if a job applicant appeared at the gate, having found Clark on his own, without help from bureaucrats or social workers, the company could not consider hiring him. No matter how eligible he seemed, nor how convincing his credentials as a member of the hard core might be, he would have to be asked to apply to a CEP office for screening.

After a few months of operations, Williams came to the conclusion that CEP procedures, and the civil servants who enforced them, were unnecessarily rigid. "They're hostile to businessmen," said Clark's personnel director, complaining about CEP's unwillingness to delegate authority for screening applicants to his own staff. "Every last one of our employees has to receive their blessing."

CEP staff members had another point of view. The female manager of the agency's makeshift field office, located in a trailer parked on the main street of the city's largest slum neighborhood, said that her biggest problem with corporate personnel representatives was caused by their attempts to hire the cream of the hard-core candidates in the area, and to reject all others. "They've disappointed a good many people already depressed," she said. According to her, personnel officials have a hard time suppressing their natural inclination to take the stronger rather than weaker applicants. "Some people think it naïve to expect company men to behave otherwise," she said. "But that's what the government gives them subsidies for, to compensate them for restraining their business instincts."

Williams knew that in order to succeed at Clark, he would have to serve two conflicting objectives: those of business and those of social work. "I sat at my desk many nights those first few months worrying about how I would maintain output rates, meet customer demands, and maintain a budget, while at the same time remain mindful of the problems and needs of the people for whom the company was created." An experienced supervisor of skilled workers, he had always had the freedom to reprimand, reassign, or fire a recalcitrant employee in order to maintain productivity. Now, he realized he would have to adjust to a new set of standards. Part of his job, for the first time in his experience, was training, counseling, and even, as some people were to put it in the weeks ahead, "spoon-feeding and coddling" his work force. Could the job be done? To supply an affirmative answer, he would certainly need a lot of help—from Planet and the "stepbrothers" in the operating divisions; from his staff of supervisors and foremen; and from the teachers who were hired to provide basic skills education. And finally, he would need help from the disadvantaged employees.

MEETING THE CHALLENGES

Williams identified three challenges to be met at Clark: (1) providing proper orientation and training for supervisors; (2) meeting the development needs of the workers; and (3) ensuring adequate economic support from Planet's divisions.

Providing Orientation for Supervisors

Williams's first major decision at Clark was responsible for tension and turmoil among the staff. With Dunsany's approval, he elected to subject the new staff members, including himself, to a short course of sensitivity training and psychological counseling. "I suppose I might have been trying to delay the start of operations," he said later. "But I really thought it would be helpful to bring a psychologist in. We were all anxious about what life would be like when the disadvantaged workers arrived. Furthermore, none of us had ever functioned in an environment where whites were the minority group."

Williams got the idea for the psychology sessions from friends at Planet. In the aerospace industry, as well as in other high-technology industries, many companies have experimented with new approaches to personnel relations intended to increase productivity and strengthen motivation. The use of a company psychologist— or even an entire department of psychologists—is no longer novel. The idea of putting clinical counselors to work is finding new

91

support among companies hiring disadvantaged workers. In fact, a whole new market has opened up for practitioners of the faddish art, a market encouraged, it should be added, by the government's willingness to cover the costs of counseling services.

Williams hired a psychologist from Planet's Arcane Division, who met with the staff during half-day sessions, three times a week for two weeks. By the end of that time, it was already clear that the experiment had failed. The sessions angered some staff members and led to the resignation of a foreman. Seven out of twelve participants wanted Williams to forget the whole idea; two suggested that a different psychologist was needed. "It was rough going," recalled one shop foreman, "they kept bringing up the question of race." The foreman who quit told Williams that he had come to Clark "to work, not enter a mental clinic." Staff members felt that their privacy was being violated, and resented it. They were made uncomfortable by the psychologist's questions about their feelings toward one another. Probably with justification they preferred to keep their feelings to themselves.

Williams, faced with so much disapproval, sent the psychologist back to Arcane. But he had not yet lost his faith in psychology as the necessary element in the new enterprise. He blamed his staff, not the therapist. "I genuinely believed the theories I had read in management magazines," he said later.

He tried one more time. After the first group of disadvantaged workers was brought in, he hired another psychologist, Dr. James Olsen, who was assigned to spend an afternoon a week at Clark, consulting to staff members and foremen about their problems in supervision. Unlike his predecessor, Olsen was not to explore the innermost feelings of the staff. He was asked to limit himself to work-related problems, advising supervisors about how to control the anger they might feel with employees who were slow learners, or how to express disapproval of defiant behavior without provoking more defiance.

Why did Williams engage Dr. Olsen? He thought he had to. He had been told by so many people—Dunsany, Button, and various

well-wishers—that the human relations problem would be stagger-
ing. The literature about programs for the disadvantaged encouraged and seemed to mandate psychological counseling, and even
implied that it is essential. He wanted to do what was called for,
to be in step with the fashions in programs for the disadvantaged.

Yet four months later he terminated Olsen's employment. "I
found the role difficult, and I guess he didn't find me very useful,"
Olsen later said. "I drifted around the plant during my visits, trying to be as informal as possible. The chief of operations thought
I was too informal. He seemed to think I ought to be filing reports on people." Olsen claimed that Williams, not his staff, needed
help. "The poor guy had the greatest burden: running the business, worrying about the staff, keeping an eye on the trainees,
answering to Planet, giving interviews to reporters. But of course,
I was not there to treat him. And I felt that if I were seen with
him too often people would distrust me."

According to Olsen, Williams soon reached a point where he
sought to avoid being "feelings-oriented." He "worried about the
employees a great deal, but also worried about worrying about
them. He wanted to prove he could be a businessman, and didn't
want to be thought of as a 'bleeding heart.'"

Williams told the staff that psychologists were an expense that
Clark could not afford. The company would have to be more cost-
conscious than it had been, he said, for a new phase had begun.
"Start-up phase is over; from now on, we all have to think business." He brought in a new assistant for personnel, and directed
him to draw up a list of rules to encourage economy. Psychology
would be replaced with business discipline. Supervisors were told
to be businesslike in their relationships with employees.

Williams admitted that he had changed his attitude toward the
workers, and had become less patient with their problems, and less
interested, too. "I had no choice," he said. "I saw that economics
was the main challenge, not psychology, and I was determined to
meet it." Olsen was probably right in saying that his job had become a luxury that had to be eliminated. "I was seen as a coddler

of the workers, even as a destructive force. I was a foreign object which the organism had to expel."

The transformation in Williams's attitude is typical of the change experienced by many managers of programs for the disadvantaged. In start-up or planning phases, they can afford to be preoccupied with issues of human relations and psychological counseling. These preoccupations are encouraged by the rhetoric about the problems of the disadvantaged, as well as by the anxiety they naturally feel when faced with a set of unknown problems. But once the workers arrive, and the business has to be run, the demands of the balance sheet are bound to take over, and sometimes it is just as well. "Sensitivity training in business isn't phony," said Williams's assistant. "It's authentic. It's an authentic distraction from the real issues."

Meeting the Special Needs of the Hard Core

"We want to emancipate people from the ghetto by providing them with an economic key," Dunsany said in a press conference. All the men and women hired by Clark met the Labor Department's definition of hard-core, or disadvantaged, candidates. According to this definition, they were "poor persons who did not have suitable employment and who were either: (1) school dropouts; (2) under twenty-three years of age; (3) forty-five years of age or over; (4) handicapped; or (5) subject to special obstacles to employment." Among the "special obstacles to employment" are race or ethnicity, functional illiteracy, and arrest records. Most corporate personnel officers assert that the hard-core worker's life-style constitutes another obstacle to employment.

The data about Clark's employees throw some light on conditions in the slum neighborhoods from which they came:

- Fifty percent of the males had arrest records, and a number had a history of drug use.
- Only 38 percent had been graduated from high school.

- Only 24 percent scored above sixth-grade levels on reading tests.
- Fifty percent were black.
- Fifty percent were Spanish-speaking.
- Nineteen percent could not speak English.
- Most had been unemployed for at least 6 months, and 20 percent were receiving public assistance when hired.
- Most were not married, though they were heads of households or primary wage earners for their families.
- Their average age was twenty-six.

In the early days of prejob training for the first group of hires, it became clear that job training would not be enough. The workers needed practical advice about their day-to-day problems, some of them work-related, some personal.

- A mother of six children, employed for the first time, was constantly preoccupied by worry about her children, who were at home alone.
- The father of a school dropout sought advice about vocational training opportunities for his son.
- A young woman wanted help in coping with her narcotics habit.
- A man who was two hours late on his first three mornings admitted that because he didn't have carfare, he had to walk ten miles every day to and from home.

To train all the new employees as quickly as possible, a product line was chosen that called for tasks that could be performed easily by both women and men and would not require high-pressure deadlines. After having mastered these tasks, employees would be offered opportunities to advance within Clark and, later, to jobs in Planet's divisions.

Clark would furnish services and products in seven skill areas: Typing; keypunching and verifying; drafting and detailing; manufacturing plastic notebook covers and binders; tool grinding; machine repair; and carpentry, including producing packing cases.

In addition to selecting the right product line, Clark tried to meet the special training needs of the employees by developing programs in three areas: vocational training, morale-building, and basic skills training.

Vocational Training. Specially designed training programs were set up. Job training, offered in a prejob phase as well as on the job, was accompanied by training in basic skills (reading, writing, and arithmetic). Planet's managers learned that their assumptions about industrial training were not always applicable to the special needs of Clark workers. New techniques were developed.

All job training was work-related. The uses of the subsidiary's products were explained to employees. "Our people want real work. They want useful things to do, not just training," said Williams. Learning was accomplished by "showing, doing, and repeating." And peer discipline and support—"the buddy system"— was used to encourage group spirit in shops and offices.

Morale-Building. Ever since Williams's disillusionment with sensitivity training and psychology, the subsidiary has been run without the services of professional counselors or therapists. The only staff member with day-to-day responsibility for ministering to the emotional needs of trainees is a registered nurse who was originally employed merely to dispense medical services, not psychological first aid. Her office became the treatment center for emotional problems, and it is busy all day. "I guess I'm the mother figure," she said. "I supply a pat on the back, a bit of advice, and, when necessary, even a loan to someone who wants to take a cab home on a rainy day." Whatever her talents, the nurse is an amateur, and some observers have suggested the need for a professional social worker. But Williams feels that Clark cannot afford the additional overhead that a social worker's salary would entail. Nor is he convinced that he would avoid a recurrence of the kinds of problems he had with his psychologists if he employed a social worker.

But the fact is that Clark's managers and supervisors have been able to cope with most morale problems. They know that employees' behavior and performance will sometimes be discouraging. "At the end of every day, our people go back to the slum to cope with life there after a hard day's work. They have more reason to be discouraged than we do."

The foremen say that they have learned to understand their employees' problems. Workers who once reported in hung over from drugs or drink after a weekend, or who did not show up after payday have learned new ways, even though Clark no longer offers sensitivity sessions or formal counseling. Staff members not only occasionally lend money to employees, they also intervene in family emergencies.

The company developed a philosophy for disciplining workers and ensuring plant security that was responsive to the problems and needs of the trainees. Williams aimed at creating an environment that he called "supportive but not indulgent." The emphasis is on work, and on the importance of learning to work satisfactorily regardless of one's personal difficulties. Soon after the departure of the second psychologist, Williams issued a list of rules—including thirty-three "thou shalt nots," such as, engaging in horseplay, scuffling, throwing things, gambling, sleeping on the job, fighting, and immoral conduct. (The list was eventually reduced to include only a few essentials, to satisfy the criticism that it was too punitive. "I was too rigid in that period," said Williams, "too worried about the need for discipline. Then I learned indirect techniques of control.")

Basic Skills Training. Eleven classes in reading, writing, and basic arithmetic supplement on-the-job training and psychological counseling. There are classes in English for Spanish-speaking workers. Half of the work force attends remedial classes one hour daily at full pay.

One continuing problem is rivalry for the time and attention of trainees between the two classroom teachers who conduct basic skills courses, on the one hand, and the shop foremen, on the other. The teachers, both women, complained during interviews that foremen have a tendency to press their employees to cut classes and stay on the production line. "These guys have to learn how to make a living; then they can learn to read," said a foreman. "We're trying to teach them," said Miss Pointer, who is in charge of the English-language classes for Spanish-speaking employees. "They're only interested in getting them to produce. It's the age-old conflict between human values and business." But both sides admitted that employees probably gain something from being fought over by everyone.

EVALUATION

The record after two and a half years shows that Clark helped employees acquire production skills and cope with personal problems that had previously been paralyzing. Success was achieved largely without formal counseling. In 1970, nearly 150 employees were on the payroll, all of whom had been certified by CEP as hard core. They included: twelve staff assistants (secretaries in the shipping and receiving and clerical departments); seven typists; eighteen draftsmen; forty-three keypunch operators (operating on three shifts); fifteen woodshop fabricators; twenty-one plastics fabricators; six tool-grinding machine operators; and twenty machine shop operators.

Absentee rates, high in the first months of operations, were at 7 percent, a bit lower than the local industry average. Turnover, however, continues at the high rate of 46 percent, 15 percentage points above average industry figures for unskilled workers. A few employees left the company for jobs elsewhere, and two had been promoted to skilled jobs in Planet's divisions.

Economic problems in the parent company's industry affected the achievement of some of Clark's goals. Thus Clark promoted only two employees to higher paying jobs in other divisions of Planet. It will be recalled that the company's MDTA proposal had stated that Clark's employees would "progress to jobs in our operating divisions upon reaching the threshold skill level on a job availability basis." But few jobs opened up in the other divisions. Total employment in Planet Corporation began steadily to decline about a year after Clark's creation, as a result of the slowdown in the national economy, and serious setbacks in aerospace.

Clark employees say that they are satisfied with their experiences in the company. In a recent attitudinal survey conducted by a team of consultants, 90 percent of the trainees indicated that Clark is "a good place to work." Data collected showed that 75 percent of the workers had developed confidence in themselves and were optimistic about their future as wage-earners.

But problems remain. Though Clark managers feel they have made much progress toward meeting the social aims of the project, they are worried about meeting the other goal: achieving success as a business enterprise. Clark had not achieved its financial objectives by the end of its second fiscal year. While expenses were generally on target, the volume of work orders received was considerably below planned levels. Direct labor hours generated were only 150,000—38 percent below expected levels. Failure to meet these levels resulted in an overhead rate of $9.20 per direct labor hour against a goal of $6.00.

Clark incurred training costs estimated at $566,000 during the second year. After reimbursements under the MDTA contract, Planet had to cover approximately $210,000 of these costs. But the true cost to the parent company was difficult to determine. It may have been more or less than the estimate depending on whether the goods and services purchased by the division from Clark were at prices in excess of or lower than fair market value. Costs to the divisions would be affected by the prices they had to pay, and would thereby affect the final tally of Planet profits, which are computed from a mix of fixed price and cost-type business, and cost-share ratios that are carried by each division.

The major economic problem was Clark's failure to obtain sufficient work orders to meet its sales goals. Purchasing agents in the parent divisions were reluctant to do business with Clark for the following reasons:

- Planet executives found it increasingly difficult to support Clark in the midst of a declining market. Their needs for the products available from Clark were not as great as originally anticipated. In some instances, they were afraid they would have to lay off some of their own employees (typists and key-punchers) in order to provide work for Clark.
- In some cases, Clark's prices were 10 to 15 percent higher per item than prices on the same goods available from other vendors in the area. High prices were caused, as everybody knew, by lower than average worker productivity.
- They had developed relationships with salesmen from other companies over the years and found it hard to turn away old friends to favor the new, experimental subsidiary.
- In its first months of operation, Clark's management did not fully realize the importance of developing their own market-ing capability. They had relied on President Button's mandate to division heads to generate business. Only after two years of operation did Clark take two important steps to carry its message to purchasing agents in the divisions and to other prospective buyers:
  —A brochure describing products and services, and the social goals of the subsidiary, was prepared.
  —A marketing unit was created within the subsidiary to so-licit orders and develop business. Clark's board of direc-tors recently acceded to Williams' request for permis-sion to look for business outside the parent company.

CONCLUSIONS

Any public-spirited businessman, no matter how strong his social conscience, will have his patience and the firmness of his commit-ment severely tried when he decides to embark on a hard-core hiring program. The key problem in such programs is the need to balance two essential goals: running a sound business while providing for the needs of disadvantaged employees. It is not an easy problem. Any subsidiary needs to produce items that are salable, to operate at a production level that is economically sound, and to attain competitive cost levels in order to offer competitive prices. But because it is committed to training and retraining its workers, and to being patient with their problems, it cannot resort to techniques traditional to business—laying off employees when production orders decline, or penalizing or firing them if they fail to meet production quotas.

This study has suggested other problems at Clark. But it must be remembered that the project is not yet three years old and, further, that it was among the first of its kind. Added costs are not unreasonable, nor are threats to the morale and attitudes of regular employees, public relations risks when programs fail or cause frictions in the community, high turnover rates, and bureaucratic inconveniences when government aid is accepted.

Another potential problem is conflict with union leaders. Such conflict was avoided at Clark because the union agreed not to organize the subsidiary's employees. But if subsidiary begins to compete successfully with plants that are unionized, thereby threatening union jobs, objections are sure to be voiced by the union.

Though Clark is still a losing proposition financially, it is nonetheless a significant achievement. Jobs and realistic vocational training have been provided to over two hundred people who had never before had successful work experiences. Black engineers and supervisors have learned about management problems in industry, and white supervisors have learned something, too, as they acquired new training skills. In addition, the parent company has won the support and friendship of community groups in a city where there is much hostility to the rest of the corporate world. Finally, there are other intangible gains to Planet, not the least of which is that its reputation for corporate citizenship has been enhanced in the eyes of the government, on whom it continues to depend for important contracts.

Clark Corporation Balance Sheet, May 31, 1969

(in thousands of dollars)

Assets		
Current Assets:		
Cash	$ 3	
Accounts receivable	89	
Inventories	80	
Prepaid expenses	2	
Total current assets		$174
Property:		
Leasehold improvements, equipment, etc.	408	
Less accumulated depreciation and amortization	107	
Net property		301
Total		$475
Liabilities		
Current Liabilities:		
Notes payable to Planet Corporation	$200	
Accounts payable and accrued liabilities	40	
Federal income taxes	(4)	
Total current liabilities		$236
Intercompany Accounts:		
Planet Corporation		(255)
Shareholders' Equity:		
Capital stock	1	
Paid in surplus	499	
Retained earnings	(6)	
Total shareholders' equity		494
Total		$475

Clark Corporation Income Statement, for eight months ended May 31, 1969

(in thousands of dollars)

Sales		$1,124
Cost of Sales		
Direct Labor Charged	$196	
Direct Material	54	
Other Direct Costs	9	
Total direct costs	$259	
Overhead Expenses		
Salaries and wages	$910	
Depreciation and amortization	82	
Building and equipment rentals	62	
Other	101	
Less federal reimbursable training expenses	230	
Net overhead expenses	$925	
Less Increase in Work-in-Process Inventories	$(60)	
Total cost of sales		1,124
Operating Profit		0
Interest Expense		9
Net Income Before Taxes		$ (9)
Federal Income Taxes		(4)
Net Income		$ (5)

8

Big Business and Urban Problems

"Big business, in America, is almost wholly devoid of anything even poetically describable as public spirit. It is frankly on the make, day in and day out . . ."

—H. L. Mencken (1924)

"Any successful businessman has to have at least enough common sense to recognize that whatever threatens the country threatens him and his family and his business."

—Henry Ford II (1970)

The optimism of businessmen about their abilities to relieve the nation's urban problems has been tempered as a result of their recent experiences. Most corporations that tried to meet the challenges of urban affairs activities, whether by setting up special manpower programs, expanding their training facilities, revising donations policies, or investing in slum economic development programs, have encountered difficulties. Few corporate executives interviewed said they felt that they had made more than a minimal contribution to solving the problems that seem even more urgent today than three years ago, when most of industry's programs were inaugurated. The economic recession has added to the woes of businessmen who set out to do some good for the cities. Urban affairs budgets must now be scrutinized more rigorously than before, as probable benefits are measured against actual costs.

Industry's publicly subsidized manpower programs are also affected by cutbacks in federal, state, and local budgets. In the fiscal year ending in June 1970, the Labor Department invested only $175 million in the JOBS program instead of the $420 originally committed,[1] and only 46,723 trainees were enrolled in the NAB's JOBS effort,[2] though employment of 338,000 disadvantaged Americans had been pledged for that date. The Labor Department's allocations for the JOBS program were trimmed for fiscal year 1971, as the department announced a reduction in funds from $340 million to $200 million.

The National Urban Coalition, industry's other voluntary organization for addressing the urban crisis, has also faced difficulties. Two years after the Coalition's formation, the *New York Times* reported that Coalition efforts had been successfully organized in only five of the thirty-two cities originally identified as urgently in need of them. In many cities interest waned rapidly among the important members of Coalition committees. Top executives went to initial meetings and soon lost interest (perhaps with good reason). They began to designate second- or third-string executives as substitutes at meetings. The Coalition idea has not lived up to its promise to inspire participation among leadership groups and to create effective action programs.[3]

As industry's efforts have lagged and as some top executives have been mouse-trapped by economic constraints or government cutbacks, the symptoms of the urban crisis, particularly unemployment among blacks, have intensified. In the Watts section of Los Angeles, for example, unemployment rose from 10.2 percent

[1] U.S. Congress, Senate, Committee on Labor and Public Welfare, *Report on the JOBS Program*, 91st Cong., 2nd sess., April 1970.

[2] U.S., Congress, Senate Committee on Labor and Puplic Welfare, Employment and Training Opportunities Act of 1970, *Report*, 91st Cong., 2nd sess. August 20, 1970, p. 9.

[3] *New York Times*, October 29, 1969.

at the time of the 1965 riots to 16.2 percent at the end of 1969, according to Labor Department reports released in August 1970.[4] The jobless rate among black women in Watts nearly doubled between 1965 and 1969.[5]

Though political problems and cost constraints provided obstacles to industry's urban affairs efforts, fault can also be found in the judgments made and strategies chosen by top companies. Hiring programs impulsively announced and inadequately conceived, training programs that isolate and divide groups of workers rather than educate and unite them, and commitments to provide upgrading opportunities based on unrealistic assumptions about available jobs, have led to disappointment among managers as well as workers who were supposed to be helped. In addition, infatuation with pseudo-psychological instruments (sensitivity training, T-groups, "urban orientation," or "organizational therapy") has sometimes caused, rather than eliminated, misunderstandings among employees and their supervisors. Moreover, these faddish programs have added to the costs of manpower training.

Industry's manpower programs have been marked by many other limitations.

1. Jobs for the disadvantaged have turned out to be at least as insecure as other jobs in industry, especially during a business recession. While promises to hire the hard core were made and kept by hundreds of large companies, commitments to keep people on the payroll were soon broken, most noticeably in aerospace, motor vehicle manufacturing, and other labor-intensive industries hit by economic problems.

3. Industry has paid little attention to job creation. As a result, unemployment or lack of advancement is still a problem, but now affects different groups of workers. In some companies, blacks have been given jobs formerly held by whites, and the latter have been laid off.

4. Personnel managers continue to have a narrow understanding of the meaning of manpower development. Large companies have

[4] *Wall Street Journal*, August 10, 1970.
[5] *Ibid.*

tremendous potential as educators of their employees. Yet, with only a few exceptions (such as New Jersey Bell and Pacific Telephone and Telegraph), corporations have not crossed the bridge from narrowly defined *training* to a broadly conceived *education* role. Only for professional employees do many large companies provide genuine educational opportunities. Subsidized tuition programs, sabbaticals for self-improvement, conferences, and weekend training programs could be offered to clerical and production, as well as to professional, workers. Industry will never discover what talent its low-level employees possess until it creates conditions that will enable their abilities to be identified and developed.

5. Special recruitment and training programs for the disadvantaged have aroused resentment among some blue and white collar workers. The double standard in hiring and promotion policies has naturally led to bitterness and to what Sar Levitan has called "blue collar blues." Clumsily devised and insensitively administered training programs have provided blacks as well as whites with justifiable grievances.

Many of the above limitations result from program conceptions formulated by government officials or policy demands made on industry by private interest groups. Accordingly, it would be unreasonable to attribute all the defects of industry's programs to corporate managers. Businessmen who have responded without careful thought to current fashions, or who only now are suspending prejudices and practices considered acceptable a few years ago, can be blamed for their amorality and other-directedness. But business-watchers who forced industry into rapid development and implementation of new programs must share the blame for the deficiencies of the new programs. In the absence of a clearly articulated and coordinated national manpower policy, industry's programs will always be open to criticism, and always found wanting.

Many corporate leaders interviewed in this study were distressed by their failure to conquer problems brought to their attention only a few years ago. Their disappointment, though understandable (most executives expect to achieve winning track records on every project they undertake) is hardly realistic. For urban affairs is a new area of corporate involvement, with many hazards and many unpredictable obstacles. There are no magic formulas for success, no easy guidelines to follow.

If businessmen are depressed about what they haven't been able to do, they are also disappointed by what they see as waning interest on the part of the federal government. Though increased measures to provide financial aids have often been discussed (tax credits, new subsidies, guarantees of government business), few of these have yet been made available.

While there are no magic formulas, there are opportunities for business to improve its performance and, in a gradual way, even to realize some returns on investment. As yet, few companies have been able to convert urban affairs into a market for their skills and products. But corporate understanding of urban problems is likely to improve as managerial experience deepens. Effective new approaches for training employees, particularly the disadvantaged, have been developed by some companies, a few of which are marketing their services as trainers, on the basis of experience with their own employees.

This book has described only briefly industry's efforts to cope with such urban problems as air and water pollution, housing shortages, and the inadequacy of health and welfare facilities. Ambitions to remedy these problems are high in some companies, and actually inspired the formation of others. But few businessmen have had much experience in these areas. As they do, they are likely to find some of the same complications and discouragements encountered by those who attempted recruitment and training programs for the disadvantaged, or those who came up against the complex policies of community relations programs. They will discover that the central issues in community problems are political rather than technological.[6] In fact, for many urban problems we do not lack technological answers. Rather, we are constrained by our inability

---

[6] See Richard S. Rosenbloom and Robin Marris (eds.), *Social Innovation in the City* (Cambridge: Harvard University Press, 1969) for a collection of essays, mainly by business school professors and students, that propose technology as a panacea for urban problems.

to agree on who should choose the solutions, or where to apply the technology. Business might very well be able to come up with a way to build attractive low-cost public housing quickly, or an efficient and economical way to decentralize a school system, but politicians and the electorate will have to decide where the housing ought to be built, who should live in it, and what priorities should be assigned to economy and efficiency. Most of today's urban problems are moral, legal, and political problems, and tackling them promises tensions for which businessmen might not be ready, and requires the special skills and sensitivities of politicians.

Since most businessmen are amateurs in politics, and inexperienced in studying and comprehending urban problems, they probably can serve the public interest best by continuing to play a limited role in urban affairs, cleaning their own houses through expanded employment and training programs, and providing revenues for the cities through taxes and donations.

The study shows that some businessmen, perhaps the wisest ones, have chosen these alternatives. Donations to urban affairs organizations and causes have been increasing yearly. For companies unwilling to take on the challenge of devising and managing action programs, the donations route is a good way to express corporate conscience. Some companies are budgeting as much for donations to urban affairs as they would have to pay to train the disadvantaged. And it is possible that leaders of community groups and self-help operations would rather be given money to support their own programs than offered low-level jobs in large corporations.

As to cleaning their own houses, businessmen have already found that this can be satisfying and rewarding, too. The data show that some companies, through new minority group hiring programs, have found and developed new sources of manpower. In addition, the unanticipated consequences of minority group hiring programs, while deterring some companies from further action, have been a source of satisfaction to others, who welcomed changes in their own environments, not the least of which has been the relaxation and liberalization of the corporate atmosphere.

110

Though it is impossible to suggest formulas or guidelines for success in urban affairs, some important issues for managers interested in running effective programs can be identified.

KEY ISSUES FOR URBAN AFFAIRS PROGRAMS

1. *The need to arrive at realistic objectives.* Urban affairs has to be taken seriously as a corporate activity, and not seen as a sideline or hobby of one or two top executives. Accordingly, planning and analysis must be required of urban program managers. Clear statements of goals and strategies are essential. Is the major goal to increase earnings per share? Is it reputation-building? Or are urban programs meant to have a positive effect on intergroup relations in the company? Is their purpose solely to find and develop more skilled minority group workers?

2. *The need to review the range of program possibilities before selecting a strategy.* As the study shows, there are many possible routes: (1) expanded or new donations programs contributing cash, staff time and skills, or facilities to outside groups; (2) minority employment and training programs; and (3) programs to provide training, counseling, and/or upgrading opportunities for the disadvantaged. Other routes to participation include loans and other assistance to minority group businessmen, "adoption" of schools, and cooperation with local efforts to improve housing, recreation, and transportation facilities. Many businessmen made commitments to set up programs which later turned out to be inappropriate for their companies. They never realized that they could make significant contributions while choosing more convenient routes to participation.

3. *The importance of estimating resources required to achieve program objectives.* A company that wants to undertake large-scale training activities ought to begin by analyzing the kinds of jobs for which it wants to train people, the needs of the people who will be trained, and the facilities that will be required. If ongoing production activities will be affected, what steps will be

111

necessary in order to prevent slowdowns in production while training is under way? Will it be necessary to increase the number of experienced employees? What incentives will be necessary to satisfy senior employees?

4. *The need to choose an affordable program.* What will the budget allow? The business's cash flow, its stockpiles of raw materials, available plant and equipment, and the skills and attitudes of staff members will need to be assessed as they bear on urban affairs objectives. The importance of taking a hard look at economic factors needs to be stressed. Some of the nation's wealthiest corporations undertook major urban affairs commitments without facing cost considerations. "The president of the company got us into this," is a frequently heard complaint of line managers, "but he isn't helping us pay for it by revising production quotas or increasing our budgets." Tough business analysis is necessary— the courage to look at the numbers and face the fact that some approaches will cost more than the company wants to pay.

5. *The need for more understanding of the political and sociological dimensions of urban problems.* Minority group training programs, as well as efforts to relate to community groups, will have implications for the internal life of the company. Frequently, traditional personnel practices and rules governing employee behavior will have to be revised. Top executives may find their attitudes and assumptions challenged by new employees. Deference patterns will probably change, as employees seek to assert identity and personality in corporate environments that have historically resisted such assertions. Some executives will, of course, welcome the transformations that take place, but others will wish they had been warned.

6. *The need to adopt a suitable organizational arrangement.* The kind of activity chosen, the objectives being sought, the hazards that have to be avoided—all should be weighed and analyzed as decisions are made as to where in the organization chart authority will be placed, and on whose shoulders. There is a real need for realistic, informed urban affairs officers. Too many companies

have given the assignment to men who did not have the confidence of top management for carrying out other corporate activities, or to energetic young amateurs, who simply haven't learned enough about the complexities of urban affairs.

Finally, corporate managers should remember that there are many opportunities to participate in the fight against urban problems without establishing formal programs or donating money and staff time. Significant participation can be achieved by reappraising and then revising deposit, purchasing, and distribution practices, and the selection of plant and facility locations. A company can have impact by changing its ways of doing business, and by attempting to influence attitudes and practices by setting an example in its own industry and in the communities it serves.

One of the lessons we have learned about the problems of the cities in the few years since publication of the Kerner Report is that they will surely be with us for a long time. Some, of course, have always been with us. Poverty, unemployment, crime, slums, even narcotics addiction, and pollution of the environment have provided grist for the mills of polemicists since the 18th century. It is the idea of impending doom from an urban crisis that is modern. But probably modern, too, is the willingness of top business leaders to plead guilty to the charge of having helped to cause the crisis, as well as their eagerness, whatever the reason, to demonstrate the existence of corporate conscience.

Guidelines for Initiating Subsidiary Training Programs

Though industry's experience in setting up and operating subsidiaries for hiring and training the hard core is still quite limited, the study of Clark suggests several key requirements for running effective subsidiaries. The following guidelines may serve as a useful checklist for managers. To the uninitiated, they offer a step-by-step procedure for establishing a subsidiary, while avoiding some of the possible pitfalls.

ESTABLISHING THE SUBSIDIARY

Managers should pay particular attention to three areas: (1) the need for support by top executives and assignment of appropriate financial and administrative resources; (2) the need for adequate planning; and (3) the need for satisfactory training arrangements.

Providing Management Commitment and Resources

Top executives must be involved from the beginning of the project in defining goals for the subsidiary and broadcasting these goals throughout the company. Executives at the highest levels must support the effort. Without their commitment, other company participants will not fully cooperate.

It is important to appoint as manager of the subsidiary someone with a reputation for getting things done. He should be familiar with the industry, and skillful in solving business problems. Urban affairs experience may be less important than business know-how. His appointment should signify to observers the importance attached by the parent company to the new project.

Demanding Thorough Preplanning

Comprehensive, fact-based, and realistic planning is essential. Planning should begin with a full exploration of alternative programs, in order to select the right approach. The operations, experiences, and problems of other subsidiaries should be reviewed.

Realistic cost, timing, and size objectives must be established. At the minimum, the following factors should be considered:

- Company investment (money, equipment, and manpower).
- Criteria for setting production timetables.
- Number of workers needed to meet production plans.
- Training needs and costs (e.g., trainers and training material).
- Costs of counseling and basic skills education.

Making the Initial Arrangements

A number of operational decisions and actions are required in setting up the subsidiary. The most important are:

- Deciding whether or not to seek government subsidies. If government assistance is to be sought, careful study of operating requirements and recruitment procedures must be undertaken.
- Securing union support.
- Training and orienting supervisors and co-workers.
- Identifying recruiting sources (private or public agencies, CEP, etc.).

In addition to providing for training needs, top management must also anticipate community reactions. Because setting up a subsidiary may provoke community problems, executives should, if possible, meet community leaders and become aware of agencies and services available in the neighborhood.

OPERATING THE SUBSIDIARY

Once the program is launched, top management must be as attentive to its progress and problems as it would be toward any other new venture. Monthly reports containing quantitative as well as other data should be required of the subsidiary's staff.

Defining Operating Characteristics

In order to assure adequate work orders, product lines should be selected with care. For products to be sold to the parent company, marketing efforts on the part of the subsidiary may not be critical. But prospective purchasers in the parent company will need economic incentives if they are to buy from the subsidiary. For goods to be sold outside the parent company, marketing know-how is essential. Product lines will have to be attractive, and satisfy existing demands.

An adequate control and reporting system must be set up to call attention quickly to problem areas. Manpower needs and production costs should be two focal points of this system.

Providing Other Services

An important component of the project will be adequate morale-building. Though psychologists or social workers are probably not needed, provisions will have to be made for assisting trainees with problems in their personal lives. It might be advantageous to hire some workers with experience, who could act as guides or coaches, and offset a feeling that bothered some Clark employees—that the subsidiary is a dumping ground for society's rejects.

It is important, too, that the program provide for transferring workers, once they are qualified, to jobs in the parent company, or with other employers.

Additional Readings

Alonso, William. "The Mirage of New Towns," *The Public Interest*, no. 19 (Spring 1970), pp. 3–17.

Banfield, Edward C. *The Unheavenly City.* Boston: Little, Brown and Company, 1970.

Becker, Gary S. *The Economics of Discrimination.* Chicago: University of Chicago Press, 1957.

Berg, Ivar (ed.). *The Business of America.* New York: Harcourt, Brace & World, 1968.

————. *The Great Training Robbery.* New York: Frederick A. Praeger, 1970.

————. "Rich Man's Qualifications for Poor Man's Jobs." *Trans-Action*, Vol. 6, No. 5 (March 1969), pp. 45–50.

Blumberg, Philip I. "Corporate Responsibility and the Social Crisis," *Boston University Law Review*, vol. 50, no. 2 (Spring 1970), pp. 157–210.

Brown, James K. "Arcata Investment Company: The Prototype 'Mesbic,' " *The Conference Board Record*, April 1970, pp. 57–64.

Carr, Elliott C. *Better Management of Business Giving.* New York: Hobbs, Dorman & Company, 1966.

Cohn, Jules. "Big Business and Slum Development," *Economic Development in Central Cities*, ed. James A. Scott. New Brunswick: Rutgers University, 1970.

————. "Business and the Cities: The Challenge of the Balance Sheet," *The MBA (Master in Business Administration)*, vol. III, no. 5 (February 1969), pp. 22–25.

————. "Business and the Hard Core of the Poor," *Social Policy,* vol. I, no. 1 (April-May 1970), pp. 56–60.

————. "Is Business Meeting the Challenge of Urban Affairs?" *Harvard Business Review.* (March-April 1970), pp. 68–82.

————. "The New Business of Business," *Urban Affairs Quarterly,* vol. 6, no. 1 (September, 1970).

Cross, Theodore L. *Black Capitalism.* New York: Atheneum, 1970.

Demaree, Allen T. "Business Picks Up the Urban Challenge," *Fortune,* April 1969, pp. 103–4, 174–84.

Derthick, Martha. *The Influence of Federal Grants.* Cambridge, Mass.: Harvard University Press, 1970.

Dickinson, Frank G. (ed.). *Philanthropy and Public Policy.* New York: National Bureau of Economic Research, 1962.

Doeringer, Peter B. *Programs to Employ the Disadvantaged.* Englewood Cliffs, N.J.: Prentice-Hall, 1969.

Eells, Richard. *Corporation Giving in a Free Society.* New York: Harper, 1969.

Ford, Henry II. *The Human Environment and Business.* New York: Weybright and Talley, 1970.

Ginzberg, Eli. "Manpower Research," *Manpower,* December 1969, pp. 3–5.

Greeley, Andrew M. *Why Can't They Be Like Us?* New York: Institute of Human Relations Press, 1969.

Grinher, William J., *et al.* Climbing the Job Ladder. New York: E. F. Shelley & Co., 1970.

Heimann, John G. *The Necessary Revolution in Housing Finance.* Washington: Urban America, Inc., 1967.

Herzberg, Frederick. "Motivating Your Employees," *Industry Week,* May 18, 1970, pp. 38–39.

————, *et al. The Motivation to Work.* New York: John Wiley & Sons, 1964.

————. *Work and the Nature of Man.* Cleveland: The World Publishing Company, 1966.

Hodgson, James D., and Brenner, Marshall H. "Successful Experience: Training Hard-Core Unemployed," *Harvard Business Review,* September-October 1968, pp. 148–56.

Janger, Allen R., and Shaeffer, Ruth G. *Managing Programs to Employ the Disadvantaged.* New York: National Industrial Conference Board, 1970.

Johnson, Lawrence A. *Employing the Hard-Core Unemployed.* New York: American Management Association, 1969.

Kalish, James A. "Urban Problems Industry," *Philadelphia Inquirer,* November 23, 1969.

Levine, Irving M. "Government's Role in Response to Needs of America's Lower Middle Class." New York: American Jewish Committee, 1969. (Mimeographed.)

————. "A Strategy for White Ethnic America." Paper presented at the Philadelphia Conference, June 1968. New York: American Jewish Committee, 1968.

Levitan, Sar A., Mangum, Garth L., and Taggart, Robert, III. *Economic Opportunity in the Ghetto.* Baltimore: The Johns Hopkins Press, 1970.

McGarr, John D., Jr. " 'Hire the Unemployables'—Corporate Slogan or Planned Program," *Labor Law Journal,* October 1969, pp. 646–66.

Mars, David. "Nixon's New Federalism," *Nation,* April 13, 1970, pp. 435–37.

Mason Edward S. The Corporation in Modern Society. Cambridge, Mass.: Harvard University Press, 1960.

Miller, S. M., and Roby, Pamela. *The Future of Inequality.* New York: Basic Books, 1970.

Morgan, John S. *Business Faces the Urban Crisis.* Houston: Gulf Publishing, 1969.

National Advisory Commission on Civil Disorders (Kerner Commission). *Report.* New York: Bantam Books, 1968.

National Industrial Conference Board. *Education, Training, and Employment of the Disadvantaged.* New York: 1969.

Netzer, Dick. *Economics and Urban Problems.* New York: Basic Books, 1970.

Oates, James F. *Economics and Urban Problems.* New York: Basic Books, 1970.

Oates, James F. *Business and Social Change.* New York: McGraw-Hill Book Company, 1968.

Paniagua, Lita, and Riessman, Frank. "New Careers in Industry," in *Up From Poverty,* ed. Frank Riessman and Hermine I. Popper. New York: Harper & Row, 1968, pp. 277–87.

Patrick, Kenneth G., and Eells, Richard. *Education and the Business Dollar.* New York: The Macmillan Company, 1969.

Quinn, Robert P., *et al. The Decision to Discriminate.* Ann Arbor: University of Michigan Institute for Social Research, 1968.

Rosen, Sumner. "Better Mousetraps," *Urban Review,* May 1970, pp. 15–18.

121

————. "Upgrading and New Careers in Health." A Paper prepared for the National Manpower Policy Task Force, March 20, 1970.

Rubel, John H. *Systems in Cities*. Washington: Urban America, Inc., 1967.

Sternlieb, George. "Hawthornism and Housing," *Urban Affairs Quarterly*, vol. 6, no. 1 (September 1970).

Thieblot, Armand J., Jr. *The Negro in the Banking Industry*. Philadelphia: Wharton School of Business and Finance, 1970.

U.S. Congress. Joint Economic Committee. *Hearings: Employment and Manpower Problems in the Cities*. 90th Cong., 2nd Sess., 1968.

——— Senate. Subcommittee on Financial Institutions of the Committee on Banking and Currency. *Hearings: Financial Institutions and the Urban Crisis*. 90th Cong., 2nd Sess., September 30–October 4, 1968.

Urban America, Inc., and The Urban Coalition. *One Year Later*. New York: Frederick A. Praeger, 1969.

Wald, George. "Corporate Responsibility for War Crimes," *New York Review of Books*, July 2, 1970, pp. 4–6.

Walton, Clarence. *Business and Social Progress*. New York: Frederick A. Praeger, 1970.

Watson, John H., III. *Twenty-Company-Sponsored Foundations*. New York: National Industrial Conferences Board, 1970.

Zimpel, Lloyd, and Panger, Daniel. *Business and the Hardcore Unemployed*. New York: Frederick Fell, Inc., 1970.